Coping with

CHANGING ROLES FOR YOUNG MEN AND WOMEN

Jessica Hanan

THE ROSEN PUBLISHING GROUP, INC.
NEW YORK

For Victoria and Madelynn, my daughters and my friends
—Love you both!

I would like to thank Madelynn Lund, Victoria Hanan, and Lance Krubner. Finally, I need to thank my editor, Amy Haugesag, for her patience and understanding.

Published in 2000 by The Rosen Publishing Group, Inc.
29 East 21st Street, New York, NY 10010

First Edition

Cover Photo by Ira Fox.

Library of Congress Cataloging-in-Publication Data

Hanan, Jessica.
   Coping with changing roles for young men and women / Jessica
      Hanan.—1st ed.
     p. cm. — (Coping with changing roles for young men and women.)
  Includes bibliographical references and index.
  ISBN 0-8239-2880-2
     1. Sex role—United States. 2. Social change—United States. I. Title.
  II. Series.

HQ1075.5.U6 H36 1999
305.3'0973—dc21

                              99-046147

About the Author

Jessica Hanan is a technical writer of text and computer-based manuals, training materials, and help documentation. She lives in Freehold, New Jersey, with her two daughters.

Contents

Introduction

Have you ever heard any of these comments?

- ➥ "Men support the family."

- ➥ "Women raise the children."

- ➥ "Math and science are not subjects for girls."

- ➥ "Guys don't have to learn how to cook, that's a woman's job."

- ➥ "Girls set the table and help with the cleaning."

- ➥ "Boys take out the garbage."

Chances are you have heard these or similar remarks. Is there any truth to these statements? There is a very good chance that you agreed with at least one of the quotes, and that illustrates how gender roles have affected your life. Several studies have shown, for example, that most teenage girls believe math is a "masculine subject." Believing this myth, having low self-esteem, and not wanting to be ridiculed by others creates feelings of incompetence in math. This type of thinking is not uncommon. Even today, many teenage girls feel that they are incapable of doing well in math, and most teenage boys will support this belief.

For teens, the transition from childhood to adulthood may create an identity crisis, causing uncertainty about who they are and what their role in society is. You and your peers are probably secure about your biological sex, but what about your gender? Gender and sex are not necessarily the same. The word *gender* means sexual identity in relation to society and culture. During your teen years, your body undergoes biological changes that can affect your emotions, self-esteem, and identity. This is a time when stereotypes about gender roles can affect your well-being.

Gender roles influence your life more than you may think. The way you are treated in school, on the job, or by authorities such as the police is directly related to your gender. Your choice of career, your participation in sports, and your preferred recreational activities are all shaped by gender roles. Gender roles can influence how you dress, your self-esteem, your dating habits, and even your choice in friends. Your entire life is affected by the role our society has determined for your gender.

Our society is patriarchal, which means that males have traditionally dominated our government, ruled the household, and determined the family lineage. A patriarchal society also expects men to provide the family with financial support, while women fulfill the function of caregiver and homemaker. This traditional line of thought feeds several myths about what women can and cannot do. A statement such as "Girls will not do well in math and the sciences" fits the image of men and women created by our society. When you analyze the traditional role of men, you can understand that they have tended to require higher salaries to support their families. Careers with more difficult math and science requirements typically pay larger salaries; therefore, men are expected to excel in these areas.

You may be asking if any of the common myths about women—such as the math and science one described above, or the myth that women are too emotional and "soft" to make good leaders—are accurate. Are gender roles solely determined by our culture? Or are they solely determined by our biological makeup? Are children taught how their gender should think, act, feel and behave? Scientists and experts agree that gender roles are shaped by three factors: culture, biology, and upbringing.

There is scientific research that can support the effect that culture, biology, and upbringing have on gender roles, and other scientific research that can deny this effect. People's lives and behavior are shaped by a multitude of sources. When a new baby is born, our culture instantly encourages gender roles for that child (female newborns are wrapped in pink blankets, male newborns in blue). From that day forward, the child's treatment by parents and family will be influenced by the child's sex. Culture *does* influence gender roles.

As a child grows, parents and educators teach certain behaviors. Some people believe that girls are supposed to wear dresses and play with dolls, whereas boys are supposed to wear pants and play with trucks. According to this view, girls are expected to be passive and gentle, but boys are expected to be aggressive and rough. Behaviors acceptable to parents in terms of how they fit the expected behavior for the child's gender are rewarded; unacceptable behaviors are punished. The child learns what role he or she should follow. Gender roles can be taught.

Anatomically, women are different from men. That is a scientific fact. Do these anatomical differences affect a person's behavior? There are scientists who believe this is true. Other scientists say that a woman's brain is different from a man's, and still others claim that female and male hormones affect a person's behavior. Though there is some disagreement about both of these concepts, many members of the scientific community agree that biological factors can determine gender roles.

You can see that gender roles can be shaped by several conditions and that gender roles influence every aspect of your life.

Earlier you read that our society is patriarchal, especially in that men work and women raise their children. Some of you—male and female—are probably thinking that this image of the family is too rigid or old-fashioned and does not reflect the reality of today's families.

In your family your mother may have a career in science, and maybe your father stays home to care for you and your sibling. This scenario is a definite possibility, but do you think it is common? If you said no, you are right— this family situation is atypical. Your family represents an example of changing gender roles.

Assigning roles based on a person's sex began centuries ago. In preliterate culture (before written history), prior to 3000 BC, women in both hunter-gatherer societies and early agricultural (farming) societies participated equally in most of the work required for the family's survival. But by the beginning of the Bronze Age, after 3000 BC, women's ability to produce new life established them as caregivers, and patriarchal societies began to develop.

However, movements during the nineteenth and especially the twentieth century sparked several changes in gender roles. Many women felt restricted by the roles that had been established for them. In the United States, several laws existed that limited women's rights. For instance, women were not allowed to vote and were denied access to most institutions of higher education. Women fought to establish their rights and their equality, which caused many to rethink the significance of gender roles.

Over time many of the changes those women wanted have become commonplace. For instance, the Nineteenth Amendment to the U.S. Constitution gave the right to vote to all women who are citizens and of legal age. Now we take this change for granted. But what about some of the more subtle changes? People now have more freedom to make choices for themselves and how they want to live their lives. Sometimes these choices can be confusing. In this book you will read about the many positive and some negative aspects of changing roles. You will learn how history has shaped changes in gender roles and how your parents' careers, behavior, and attitude toward your opposite sex sibling can affect your life. The book will explain how to deal with rigid gender roles. It will also help you cope with gender-bias challenges in education, sports, military, and social activities.

Here you will read about current dating trends, the influences gender roles have on your appearance and career choices, how you are treated in the work environment, and how the media influences gender roles. All the areas discussed can create changes that may make you feel confused, frustrated—even angry. This book will help you identify how these changes in gender roles have affected your life and help you learn how to cope.

Gender Roles
Throughout History

Terry ran into the house, threw his bookbag onto the floor, and headed for the kitchen. His mom, his sisters, and his brothers weren't too far behind. The kitchen was a flurry of activity. Mom opened the freezer and asked who wanted which entree. Terry and his siblings set their places, got their drinks, and selected their meals.

As entrees emerged from the microwave, they were placed at the table. Finally dinner was ready, and everyone sat down to eat.

Thirty minutes passed, then suddenly conversations were cut short when Terry looked at his watch and yelled, "Gotta leave for practice. See ya all later."

Terry didn't have to look back to know the events occurring in the kitchen. One by one his older sister and brothers announced their evening plans and left. Mom drove Terry's youngest sister to gymnastics.

Words such as *"hectic," "fast-paced," "active,"* and *"chaotic"* would describe the majority of modern households. Most teens and their siblings participate in several types of extracurricular activities. Like Terry and his siblings, most teenagers help both parents with chores and child care, as they have throughout most of history. Many help by working to earn extra cash and by supervising younger siblings. Today's household chores are not always determined according to sex, as they were in earlier generations. Boys today, unlike those in the past, may perform tasks, such as washing dishes or cooking, that were once thought of as "feminine," and girls may do chores, such as taking out the garbage, once thought of as "masculine."

Today, in most families, women are not only wives and mothers, but also breadwinners, either alone or with husbands or partners. Most modern women have careers, and most men share in child-rearing, housecleaning, and cooking.

Was this always true? No. In the past, society identified gender roles by sex—men had careers, whereas women stayed home to cook, clean, and raise the children. When and how did this separation of roles begin? Most primitive societies had this division of labor. Hunter-gathering societies assigned big game hunting to men because they could leave the homestead or camp to travel. Women, who were homebound because of child rearing, were delegated both domestic chores and the gathering of vegetables, small animals and birds' eggs. If you look at this split in labor, it may appear to make sense. However, in some of these societies women also performed many strenuous and demanding domestic tasks. These tasks included unloading pack animals, setting up camp, building fires, and putting up temporary homes.

Women's roles have varied throughout history depending on culture. In certain Native American cultures, for example, women determined whether captives were killed or adopted into the tribe. They also had the right to veto a declaration of war and, after proving their bravery in battle, could sit on the warrior's council. But because of women's ability to give birth and nurse children, the old domestic roles remained dominant. This stereotyping of the division of labor led to the traditional female gender role that existed in Western society for centuries. That role has only begun to change within the last century or so, and change has come slowly.

What changed in our society? Women became socially active in the movements to free slaves (abolition) and ban alcohol (temperance). These activities made nineteenth-century women begin to think about their own rights and freedom. They wanted an education, the right to vote, equal wages, and equality.

Gender roles began to change in the United States in the mid-1800s when two American abolitionists, Lucretia Mott and Elizabeth Cady Stanton, met in London. Both women, accompanied by their husbands, were in London for the World's Anti-Slavery Convention. Lucretia Mott and Henry Stanton were to serve as delegates, but Mott and other female delegates were refused participation when the controlling faction of the antislavery movement objected to women participating in public events.

Lucretia Mott and Elizabeth Cady Stanton spent much time together during their trip discussing the treatment of women. These discussions lead to their decision to create an organization to advocate women's rights. It took several years, but eventually more women joined them, and a movement developed. The first Women's Rights Convention at Seneca Falls was held in 1848. At this event, Stanton declared that "all men and women are created equal" and called for reforms in marriage, suffrage (voting rights), and inheritance laws.

Beginning in the nineteenth century, the women's movement fought for race and gender equality. Many of the issues and questions first addressed by the women in the movement are still relevant today. These women questioned their position in society as well as the institutions, organizations, and customs that maintained their status and blocked any progress toward equality. For example, these female activists questioned the views of church, state, law enforcement, marriage, schools, courts, birth control, divorce issues, inheritance, wages, and matters of property.

When the U.S. Constitution first granted voting rights, those rights were given only to white male property owners; only 6 percent of the adult male population was eligible to benefit from this privilege. As our democracy matured, religious and property qualifications were eliminated, and more white men gained the right to vote. Blacks and women, however, still could not vote. By the end of the nineteenth century, voting rights had become the focus of the women's movement and the subject of the first large-scale public demand made by women in the United States.

In 1851 Elizabeth Cady Stanton met another activist, Susan B. Anthony, and they became political partners and very good friends. While raising seven children, Stanton had been writing feminist articles from her home. With Anthony's encouragement she wrote speeches and letters to escape the boredom of housework. In Stanton's first public address since the Seneca Falls convention, she stated that drunkenness should be grounds for divorce, and that a woman whose husband is a drunkard should get custody of their children. This was a radical thought at the time, since women were expected to obey their husbands regardless of the husbands' behavior.

Both Stanton and Anthony advocated women's rights in voting, education, property ownership, earning and inheriting money, and executing their husbands' estates. They urged legislation for women's voting rights, saying the right to vote would provide women the best protection. To further their cause, Susan B. Anthony and Elizabeth Cady Stanton founded the National Woman Suffrage Association.

With the support of former slave Sojourner Truth, Anthony and Stanton refused to endorse the Fifteenth Amendment to the U.S. Constitution, which gave the right to vote to black men—but not to women, white or black. This split the movement into opposing factions and led to the creation of a new organization, the American Woman Suffrage Association. In 1890 both organizations merged to become the National American Woman Suffrage Association (NAWSA). This merger attracted educated, influential women who strengthened the growing women's movement. Activists traveled throughout the United States, Canada, and Europe promoting women's rights.

The fight for women's rights now became an international movement, and some advances were achieved. For example, women's unions were formed, higher education was becoming available, and women started entering fields that had traditionally been reserved for men (medicine and

11

law, for example). But the original demand to vote had not yet been achieved. When the United States entered World War I, in 1917, many industrial and office jobs that were left vacant by servicemen were filled by women. Arguing that women were now proving themselves equal to men, the woman suffragists battled more vigorously for voting rights. However, it wasn't until 1918 that the Nineteenth Amendment, guaranteeing women's right to vote, was passed by the House of Representatives. Finally, in 1920, the amendment was ratified, and all eligible women had the right to vote.

Not only American women won their right to vote. The woman suffrage movement affected much of Europe, Canada, parts of Asia, some Latin American countries, India, many Middle Eastern countries, and some African countries. Most of these countries granted women the right to vote between 1906 and the late 1940s. Believe it or not, Liechtenstein (a small country between Austria and Switzerland) did not grant women permission to vote until 1984.

Woman suffrage strengthened, united, and focused the women's movement. By the time women received the right to vote, most women began to realize that they could function well outside the home. These women recognized that they are as capable as men and that they wanted to continue the fight for women's equality.

But with the achievement of the right to vote, the majority of women felt they had achieved equal rights, and the momentum of the women's movement decreased. For more than twenty years, the women's movement lay dormant. Then suddenly the United States was at war again.

World War II sent men overseas and, again, women entered the workforce to help the war effort. During these years, women had access to skilled, high-paying jobs. These women began to realize that they were capable of earning high pay and that they had the skills to work in fields previously dominated by men.

Before the war effort, the majority of married women had worked in the home, taking in boarders, sewing, and laundry, and performing other domestic chores if they needed the income. When the war ended, women were expected to leave the workforce, even though 80 percent wanted to remain. Women were laid off from their wartime jobs so that returning servicemen could reclaim them. Over two million women lost the jobs they had held during wartime and were sent back to their domestic chores. Still, some women remained at work, and more entered the workforce at an increasing rate. Attempts were made to glorify women's work and to convince people that married women belonged at home caring for their husbands and children and maintaining an immaculate house. Many advertisements, magazine articles, and political debates were aimed at keeping women at home. The propaganda succeeded, and again the movement became inactive.

The women's movement was not reborn until 1953. A French woman, Simone de Beauvoir, claimed that all countries were dominated by men. She accused them of treating women as second-class citizens. Her book *The Second Sex* received international attention. Since the end of World War II, careers, even for educated women, had been frowned upon. Competing with men for jobs was seen as unattractive. Women were again feeling discontented and unfulfilled. These hidden thoughts and feelings had a profound influence on women in Western society. They were again put into words by Betty Friedan when her book *The Feminine Mystique* was published in 1963.

During the 1960s and 1970s the modern feminist movement started to take shape. Betty Friedan helped found the National Organization for Women (NOW), an organization dedicated to fighting for women's equal rights. NOW's leadership and members were well educated, had the ability and contacts to gain media attention, and were experienced political activists and lobbyists. This new feminist movement pushed for social reforms. The movement's efforts helped get the following legislation enacted:

- Equal Pay Act of 1963. This act outlawed the determination of wages based on gender.

- Civil Rights Act of 1964. Title VII of this act forbids sex discrimination in employment.

- 1964 Credit Law. This law granted women the right to receive credit. Previously, banks would not lend women money to start businesses, open professional offices, or buy homes.

- Title IX of the Education Omnibus Act of 1972. This law prohibits gender bias in any educational program or activity.

- Roe vs. Wade. This landmark U.S. Supreme Court decision overruled state laws and legalized abortion for women up to six months pregnant.

↪ Pregnancy Discrimination Act of 1978. Under this act, an employer is forbidden to fire or demote a pregnant employee.

NOW also spent years attempting to convince Congress to pass the Equal Rights Amendment, or ERA. The purpose of this proposed constitutional amendment was to make sex discrimination a direct violation of constitutional rights. The amendment was originally written in 1923 and reintroduced in Congress in 1972. It was ratified by Congress but never approved by a majority of state legislatures as required, and eventually the women's movement abandoned the fight.

Women's organizations grew in strength and became more public throughout the 1970s. Demands were made, and the importance of women voters and the issues that they cared about began to be recognized by politicians. Several groups were created to determine inequalities and lobby for new legislation. These included:

↪ The Commission on the Status of Women, which collected and presented documentation of discrimination

↪ The National Women's Political Caucus, which works to have more women elected and appointed to political positions

↪ The Women's Equity Action League, which fought for equal rights for women

↪ The Equal Employment Opportunity Commission, which provides guidelines to employers on how to follow the law and hears complaints from people who feel discriminated against

⇨ The Women's Action Alliance, which is a national center for women's programs and issues

The Feminist Movement and Gender Roles

The women's movement of the 1960s and 1970s had an enormous effect on gender roles. Women activists began to refer to themselves as feminists. These women took a more serious look at how society viewed women. Changes to gender roles began with public awareness. Prior to the movement's success, the general public believed that women had only one role. Magazines, television, and politics portrayed women as only wives and mothers. Schoolbooks told little of women's contributions to history, and the standard stereotypes about women's capabilities remained.

Feminists publicized "women's issues," which became popular with talk shows, magazines, and newspapers. Typical gender stereotypes of women as sex objects and symbols of beauty were challenged. Activists in the women's movement made the public aware that these stereotypes needed to be changed. Women began to hold jobs outside the home in large numbers. Throughout much of Western society, they began to participate in sports, received college educations, became members of the medical and legal professions, were elected to government offices, could control their ability to give birth by using birth control or through legal abortion, and were recognized as full citizens.

The women's movement made tremendous strides in modifying the female stereotype. At the same time, historical events were also changing the idea of masculinity. The "hippie" movement established a more feminine look for men: long hair, flowered shirts and accessories such as beads and earrings. Communal living arrangements, with domestic functions shared by both sexes, became popular during this time. In addition, the response to the Vietnam War led to a softening of the masculine image. Young men who protested this war were changing the definition of masculinity by declaring that behaving aggressively and waging war weren't necessary to prove their manhood. Lastly, homosexuality was becoming more public as the gay rights movement took hold. People's views of gender roles were changed forever during the 1960s and 1970s.

Gender roles continued to change. Although the Equal Rights Amendment was never ratified, it had a powerful impact on women's lives nonetheless. The fight for ratification failed in 1982, but the battle created permanent changes. Several strides were made during the 1980s that continue to have an impact today. During the 1980s, legislation against gender discrimination began to be more strictly enforced. In 1980, the Equal Employment Opportunity Commission declared sexual harassment to be an act of sex discrimination. This made sexual harassment illegal under Title VII of the Civil Rights Act.

New barriers were broken during the 1980s and have continued to be broken. Wives now have a voice in the decision to sell joint property holdings. Companies that do work or provide services for the federal government are forbidden to discriminate on the basis of sex. Single women can obtain contraceptives, giving them choices that they lacked in the past about when and whether to have babies. Women can now attend what were once all-male military schools and serve in the military in every capacity. Women can take maternity leave without losing their jobs. Women have also become more prominent in sports, in the media, and as corporate executives. The changes created by the women's movement have affected everyone. Gender role stereotypes are still being broken and redefined.

Changing Gender Roles and You

You may be wondering how these new and changing gender roles apply to you. How do changing gender roles affect your life? Well, the answer is that they influence every aspect of your life. Your family structure, education, career goals, dating techniques, sports participation, and forms of entertainment are all influenced by changing gender roles. For instance, do both your parents work? Are your parents divorced, and if they are, do you live with your father or mother? Is your guardian a single parent? These questions are just a few examples of how traditional family structure has changed.

Many things that you now consider normal or commonplace was once considered unusual and unacceptable. Changes to old standards apply in the area of education as well. The majority of schools are now coeducational, and so is most of the curriculum. But do you realize that when your parents were in school, each sex attended a separate gym class? Just a few decades ago, a woman would never

18

ask a man out on a date. Now it is usually a woman who makes the first move. How do you feel about this change? Do you think it affects how you behave?

The questions and examples you have just read illustrate the effect that the women's movement has had on gender roles and on our lives. Not all of the movement's ideals have been realized yet, and more changes in gender roles are inevitable. Changes will continually affect how society evolves, and changing gender roles will always play a part in our lives.

Family Life
and Gender Roles

Jared looked around the room. Several of his class-mates were with both of their parents. A few class-mates were with only one parent. But he was certain that the missing parent was either at work or watching younger children. Jared looked at his dad and remembered how his mom had left them a few years earlier. He remembered the embarrassment, anger, and pain he had suffered then.

Now, sitting in homeroom on back to school night, he watched parents and teens arrive. Old feelings started to return as Jared yearned to be part of a "whole family." Jared was beginning to feel very self-conscious. Finally his friend Tony walked into the room. Tony was with his mom. Right away Jared started to feel less concerned and anxious because he knew that Tony's parents had gotten a divorce five years ago. Now Jared was positive he wasn't the only guy there without a "normal" family.

What is a family? According to the *Merriam Webster's Collegiate Dictionary* (Tenth Edition), one definition of *family* is "the basic unit in society traditionally consisting of two parents rearing their own or adopted children . . ." This definition reflects society's oldest idea about families, and the type of family it describes is often termed the nuclear family. The concept of the nuclear family dates back to man's earliest ancestors and is accepted as the modern idea of family.

What about Jared and Tony? Jared thought wistfully about a "normal family." Are you a family if you only live with one parent? What about teens who live with foster families? Currently, same-sex couples are having children through adoption, artificial insemination, and other methods. Are those groups families? In addition, as the cost of living increases, groups of friends and their children are living together. Are these groups of adults and children families? Jared may not have realized it, but the "normal" family is not so normal anymore.

Modern families are diverse. More and more nontraditional lifestyles are becoming commonplace and accepted. Children and teens are being raised by caring adults in living arrangements that are not necessarily considered a traditional family setting. Does that mean these nurturing units are not families? Because of our changing society, a broader definition of family now exists. *Merriam Webster's Collegiate Dictionary* (Tenth Edition) also includes definitions of *family* that reflect current trends. They are: "a group of individuals living under one roof and usually under one head: household" and ". . . also: any of various social units differing from but regarded as equivalent to the traditional family."

Almost every one of you has been a member of a family. Your parent(s) or guardian(s) play a major role in your social, physical, and emotional development. Part of your social conditioning includes the formation of your gender role identity. As family members, your parents have the first and strongest influence on the development of your gender role identity.

Parents' Influence on Gender Roles

You read in the introduction that when babies are born, girls are wrapped in pink blankets, and boys are wrapped in blue. From that day forward your parents' behavior toward you and treatment of you is predetermined and influenced by your biological sex. Your behavior, decisions, emotions, and personality are affected by your parents in several ways. Parents teach their children by reward and punishment, parent-child interactions, reinforcement, approval and disapproval, encouragement, and by serving as role models.

When you were a toddler, your parents probably chose your toys based on your sex—dolls and stuffed animals for girls, cars and balls for boys. The way you played with these toys, your choice of friends, and how you behaved with these friends was influenced by your sex too. Playing house, tea parties with dolls and stuffed animals, jumping rope, and dancing are all considered acceptable playtime activities for young girls. Playing ball, building roads for cars and trucks, having snowball or mud fights, and creating space battles are among the activities thought to be appropriate for "normal" young boys. Parents tend to reward behaviors they believe proper for their child's sex and punish or discourage behaviors they believe improper. Each time a behavior is rewarded, it is reinforced, and so-called improper behavior is suppressed.

Some male children, for example, are congratulated when they fight a neighborhood bully. Their parents' praise reinforces the aggressive act, encouraging the child to repeat the behavior until finally it establishes aggression as a personality trait. In contrast, most female children are seen as gentle and non-aggressive. How is this behavior taught by parents? If favorable behaviors are rewarded, unwanted behaviors are punished. Girls who play rough or fight are ridiculed, called tomboys and, in most cases, punished for fighting. Unkind words from parents and parental disapproval usually cause a child to abandon the undesirable behavior and lead to the development of passive, "ladylike" personality traits.

While you were growing up, and especially now during adolescence, your parents, knowingly or unknowingly, help determine your gender role. When parents approve of certain behaviors and actions, they influence your decision to continue them. If these activities are specific to a particular gender role, they become part of your normal actions. When parents agree with the choices you make, whether in school courses, friendships, activities, or careers, their encouragement is an indication that you should continue behaving in this manner. This type of parental interaction has a significant effect on your gender identity.

Jim and his parents are discussing the electives he should take next year at school. Jim selects a technology class. Jim's father smiles and tells him it's a great choice. Happy that his father approved, Jim tells his parents that he also plans to take a food science class. Suddenly Jim's father storms out of the room, shaking his head. As his father walks away, Jim crosses out the food science class and returns to the course guide.

Jim's father didn't say a word, but his actions were a clear indication of how he felt about his son taking a food science class. Without Jim's father saying a word, this example of parent-child interaction clearly reinforced the gender stereotype that cooking is "sissy stuff."

Parents come from different cultural and educational backgrounds and varying financial situations. All of these factors affect how they raise their children. In addition the way you are treated by your parents may depend on your current family situation, which may be different from your best friend's. You know that other people, teachers, and your friends all have different habits, beliefs, and behaviors. Understand, too, that these differences exist between your mother and father. Know that these behaviors, how your grandparents raised your mom and dad, and your current family situation directly affect how your parents treat you and your siblings. The way parents establish gender role identities varies between generations and families.

When your parents were growing up, in a majority of families, the father was the sole breadwinner. The mother kept house, raised the children, and cooked meals. These stereotypes had an effect on your parents. Your parents' reaction to these conditions is reflected in their treatment of you and your siblings.

Some parents reject these stereotypes. According to the Spring 1997 issue of *National Forum* magazine, over 80 percent of Americans agree that two incomes are needed to financially support a family. Women's entry into the workforce has become perhaps the most important social trend of the last fifty years.

Do both of your parents work? Does your father help you with your schoolwork or other activities? For most people your age, the answer to these questions is probably yes. Families have changed, and so have parental roles. Women are more likely to have careers, and men are now becoming actively involved in child rearing. This type of family situation is rapidly becoming more and more common.

Have you ever heard the expression "Do as I say, not as I do"? Does the concept illustrated by this expression ever work? For most people, the answer is no. As a teen, you are much more likely to respect someone who gives you respect and follow the advice of someone that takes their own advice. This phrase and its effect on people's behavior show the value of role models. Your parents are your first and most influential role models. As role models your parents have a major effect on the development of your gender role identity.

How Your Parents' Behavior Affects You

"Actions speak louder than words." Most people have heard this statement at one time or another, and most would probably agree that it is true. Your parents' behavior toward one another illustrates the accuracy of this saying. Your parents' actions toward each other and toward you and your siblings play an important part in the development of your gender role. Their work habits and careers also affect how your gender identity develops.

Does Mom work or stay home? Is Dad or Mom the main breadwinner, or do they both support the family? Which parent spends the most time caring for you and your siblings?

Although you may not realize it, your parents' work habits and careers influence how you view your gender and how you feel about yourself. There have been some controversial recent studies, including one published in the September 1997 issue of *Youth Studies* that suggest that strict adherence to gender roles, with mothers staying home to raise the children, help instill a sense of security and facilitate decision-making skills. But this gender role stereotype also perpetuates society's unfair treatment of women, limits opportunities for both sexes, and ignores their respective talents.

Of course, not all women who are homemakers do so because of stereotyping. Many women in today's society have chosen to abandon or postpone their careers to be full-time moms. In most cases, this choice was a decision that involved both parents. When both parents have an equal, or near-equal, involvement in child care, housekeeping, and finances, they model their belief of sexual equality for their children. Parents who have this modern view of gender roles are indirectly teaching these values to their children. The same issue of *Youth Studies* mentioned previously also states that teens who learn and follow this model of gender roles develop higher self-esteem and are more flexible in dating practices and relationships.

Parents who are in nontraditional careers demonstrate that gender should not dictate future goals. If your parents provide this example, you will have more freedom to choose your career and probably more support once you have made your choice.

If your dad takes on parenting responsibilities, he is more likely to become actively involved in your life, treat you and your siblings equally regardless of sex, and help you set realistic goals. In addition, fathers (and mothers) who are involved in your upbringing will tend to listen and comfort rather than dictate or direct your actions, goals, and behaviors.

Men who choose not to be involved in parenting usually do so because they hold an older view of masculine identity. In traditional family environments, most women feel obligated to "serve" the man of the house. This atmosphere leads to the division of family work based on sex. In these situations your parents' behavior helps determine how you perceive your place in the family. When you learn that family responsibilities are classified by sex, your parents have influenced your gender role by reinforcing the gender stereotype and teaching gender inequality.

Parents' treatment of one another also influences how you treat the opposite sex. Fathers who display subtle sexist attitudes toward their wives let sons know that gender differences exist and that men are superior in some way. This subtle definition of women as second-class citizens exists in many of today's two-parent families. Women who cater to their spouses will defend this behavior to their children and insist that the children behave in the same way. This reinforces the man's privileged position in society. In doing this, these women have taught their children that men are superior and women are subservient to them.

On the other hand, some men may tell the children that they have a high opinion of their mother's qualities, but then during the course of a normal day, the children may hear their father put down or belittle their mother. Most females raised in this family environment grow up thinking they should be submissive. Living in a family situation in which there is gender tension may explain some of the hostile feelings you may have toward your parents.

In this type of family situation, you may also notice that your siblings of the opposite sex, if you have them, are treated differently. If you're male, do you notice any difference between the way your father treats your sister and the way he treats you? Are you given the freedom to express your feelings or emotions, or are you told to "take it like a man"? As a young woman, do you find that your father is more protective of you than of your brothers? Do your parents give your brothers more freedom? Does your mother treat your brother differently than you?

How Your Parents' Treatment of Opposite-Sex Siblings Affects You

Did you answer "yes" to any of the questions you read in the previous paragraph? If you did, you are not alone. The way parents treat an opposite-sex sibling definitely has an influence on your behavior, feelings, and gender role.

If you are male, do you take out the garbage? Do you have more freedom when it comes to dating and a curfew than your sisters? Are you expected to go to college, trade school, or technical school for an education that will lead to a career? And, are you allowed to cry, show emotion, or be sentimental without feeling like a "sissy"? If you are female, are you responsible for doing the dishes? Have you lost some of your freedom since you became old enough to date and stay out late? Are you expected to marry and have children? And are you taken seriously when you are angry? All these questions illustrate some typical expectations parents have for teens of each sex.

In the *Hite Report on the Family,* Shere Hite stated that:

- ↪ Eighty-three percent of girls surveyed said that their mothers gave their brothers more freedom and privileges.

- ↪ Seventy-five percent of females in their teens and twenties said that their mothers allowed their brothers to skip chores and go out more often.

- ↪ Boys were given encouragement, financial support, and college guidance for education and business advancement.

- ↪ Boys are encouraged to be active and angry.

- ↪ Girls are expected to marry.

- ↪ Teen girls are required to help clean and do housework while their brothers are allowed to have fun.

- ↪ Girls are encouraged to be loving and passive.

Is this true in your family? How do you feel about it? Feelings of anger, jealousy, unworthiness, and being unloved are just examples of the emotions teen women may experience as a result of this difference in treatment by their parents.

Why do parents treat siblings of the opposite sex differently? Nothing you did caused your parents to behave this way. Your parents may not even realize the effect this discriminatory behavior is having on your emotions and development. Remember, your parents' ideas of gender roles were developed when they were your age. They were "trained" to treat you and your siblings this way. Undoing these values and ideas is very difficult, but it can happen.

How You Can Cope with Rigid Gender Roles

Do your parents have strict ideas about gender roles? Changing your parents' way of thinking is difficult but worth trying. You can talk about modern views of gender identity. Watch television with your parents to illustrate how times have changed. Talk about your friends' families and let your parents know that there are differences in the way gender roles are perceived nowadays. By educating your parents, you may influence their views of gender roles.

Don't be surprised if this doesn't work, however. Gender role development occurs slowly over time. Parents who raise their children following rigid gender roles may not be open to change. Your best way of coping is to have patience. Remember, in a few years you will be of legal age and can follow the ideas that you believe.

Does Your Gender Influence Your Education?

Years ago, Michael's father left his mother, his three sisters, and him. Michael remembered how angry and alone he felt. When his mom was at work, he took his anger out on his sisters, forcing them to cook and wait on him. Then one day his sisters decided they would refuse to listen to his demands. No matter how Michael threatened, they all simply refused to listen. When he yelled, they just blasted the television until he couldn't be heard. Finally Michael just gave up and joined his sisters as they watched a goofy cooking show.

Michael couldn't remember how, when, or why he started listening and enjoying the show. But Michael did remember how amazed he was when he realized that most of the cooking show chefs were male. Suddenly he became fascinated with cooking. Over the next few weeks, he started to prepare meals for his sisters and mom. Michael even began to think about becoming a chef.

Last spring when Michael had to select his classes, he discussed his thoughts about being a chef with both his mom and his guidance counselor. Both adults agreed that taking a food science class would help Michael decide whether this was the right career for him.

Now, as he walked into his food science class, he

thought about the fun he would have in this "cake course." Looking around the room he noticed that there were only three other guys in the class. "Wow," he thought. "Plenty of girls! This class is going to be better than I imagined!" Michael found a seat and sat down. Before he knew it the bell had rung and class was over. Michael left the class feeling good about his choice of elective.

As Michael approached the row of lockers, he was suddenly shoved against them. Lifting his head up, the leader of a rough group of guys, shouted "Gonna bake me a cake, fag? It better be good, or next time we won't be so gentle."

Have you experienced any gender prejudice in school? Have you ever been in a class that a teacher or fellow student thought was inappropriate for your sex? If you have, you're not alone. Even today, it is uncommon to see many female teens taking advanced math and science courses— and it is just as unusual to see male teens taking chorus, sewing, or food science classes. Why do these situations occur? Because of expectations!

Expectations—what parents, family, friends, guidance counselors, and teachers feel you are capable of and qualified to do—may be determined not only by your abilities, but by your gender.

Grade School Through Post Secondary School

As a kindergarten student, you went to school to play, or so you thought. Starting in first grade, what your teachers expected of you was predetermined based on your gender. Until studies done in the early 1990s brought the issue into focus, it was widely understood that girls would not do well in math and science and would not be interested in those subjects. They were not expected to continue their education after high school, and if they did, they were expected to choose careers such as teaching, nursing, and secretarial positions. Boys, on the other hand, were expected to do well in math and science, continue their educations, attend college, and go on to become doctors, lawyers, or accountants. These expectations have held on for many years, and they were most likely transmitted to you and your peers subconsciously. Your teachers' gender biases knowingly or unknowingly influenced the way the teachers behave and their attitudes toward you. Research has shown, for example, that:

- When teaching math and science, teachers tend to call on boys more often than girls.

- Boys' answers are usually taken more seriously.

- Boys are given more feedback and attention.

- The appearance and clothing of girls frequently receive more comments.

- Boys are given more access to scientific equipment.

- Teachers tend to "talk down" to girls.

These hidden attitudes are also reflected in a teacher's treatment of skills, daily living tasks, careers, colors (giving pink or red crayons and paper to girls and blue or green to boys, for example), group names, and games.

Studies have shown that throughout your school years, gender differences influence your education. The influence your grade school teachers had on you created feelings and attitudes that affected your choice of course work in junior and senior high school.

According to findings from a report entitled *The Condition of Education 1997,* at the age of nine, boys and girls have similar levels of mathematics and science mastery. But a gender gap in science starts to appear at the age of thirteen. As you continue into high school, the gap between male and female performance and ability in both mathematics and science widens. These differences are also apparent when students take the Scholastic Aptitude Test (SAT). Men score higher on both mathematics and science achievement tests and advanced placement (AP) examinations. Why do you think these differences in achievement in mathematics and science happen?

These changes in a female student's ability in mathematics and sciences begin at about the age of thirteen (roughly the same time as puberty begins). At this age most girls are becoming concerned about their appearance and what boys think of and about them. Girls who are serious students and have an interest in and do well in mathematics and science are thought of as "nerds," "brainiacs," or "geeks." Teen girls who are considered nerds by their peers are not viewed as attractive by many teen boys. Therefore, most girls avoid elective courses in math and science. This means that the girls do not have the right preparation for higher level courses in these subjects during high school and afterward. These attitudes and the actions they cause contribute to this widened gender gap.

Performance levels in math and science vary as students progress into high school and college. Behavioral patterns established in junior high school continue through to senior high school and influence students' career choices. For instance, according to *The Condition of Education 1997*, even though an equal number of male and female high school seniors may anticipate pursuing careers in math or science, 9 percent of male seniors are likely to select engineering as a career, compared to only 2 percent of female seniors.

Today teachers are being trained to recognize their unconscious gender biases and the behavior that those biases cause. Classroom materials are being updated to include gender-neutral language and strong, positive female characteristics, and more women are being promoted into administrative positions in education. These positive improvements are helping close the gender gap exhibited in today's educational environment. And improvements are already being seen—the gender gap in mathematics between male and female seventeen-year-olds is narrowing. The differences in the science abilities of male and female students are improving as well, though not as much as in mathematics.

Although these improvements are impressive, new areas of education have created their own gender gaps. These areas are technology education and school-to-work programs (which train students for specific careers). More boys than girls tend to enroll in technology courses, and high school counselors are recommending school-to-work programs that prepare students for occupations that are traditional for their gender. As educational reforms continue to work at creating gender equality, you should be aware of how your attitudes toward these educational issues are created. Then you can begin to improve and create your own gender equality.

Many factors influence your attitudes and achievement in mathematics, science, and technology. These factors include:

➯ How well you do in math and science courses

➯ Encouragement from your parents

➯ The resources you have available at home

➯ How well your math and science teachers are prepared

➯ How you interact with your math and science teachers

➯ The curriculum content

➯ Laboratory experiences

➯ The availability of mentors and role models

Your teachers have a major influence on how you think and feel about academic subjects, including mathematics, science, and technology. Their unconscious actions and behaviors take time to change, but many teachers' attitudes are improving. Once you become aware of your own attitudes, you can use the information supplied by your teachers and guidance counselors more effectively. It is up to you to determine how their recommendations and guidance will affect your education and, in turn, your life. By making educated decisions you will help create gender equality, if not for all male and female students, at least for yourself and some of your friends.

Interestingly, some parents and educators have found that the best way to avoid imposing stereotypical gender roles on students is to educate girls and boys separately. Same-sex classes and even separate schools for each gender are becoming more common. Studies show that many girls and boys thrive in an atmosphere without pressure or competition from members of the opposite sex.

School segregation by gender is legal only for private institutions. Public schools and other institutions that receive money from the government are required to admit qualified applicants of either gender. This law has been the subject of several legal battles recently, including the well-known case of Shannon Faulkner. In 1993 Shannon applied to the Citadel, an all-male school in South Carolina. The Citadel is not affiliated with the U.S. armed forces, but it prepares students for careers in the military. Shannon did not specify her gender on her application, and she was accepted for admission. When the Citadel learned that she was female, they denied her admission. Because the Citadel receives funding from the state of South Carolina, however, Shannon believed that the refusal to allow her to attend was unconstitutional, and she sued the school to be allowed to attend. The legal battle over Shannon's admission lasted for two years and eventually reached the U.S. Supreme Court, the highest court in the country. Finally, Shannon was cleared to attend the Citadel. She became the school's first female cadet in its long history. Although Shannon withdrew from the school after only a short time, her efforts crashed one of the last remaining barriers to coeducation and paved the way for women to be admitted to the Citadel and another similar school, Virginia Military Academy.

Treatment by Educators

Earlier you read how expectations create gender bias and what effect this has on your education. Educators, guidance counselors, and educational materials also influence and help cause gender biases that in turn influence your education.

Unknowingly (and sometimes knowingly) teachers and guidance counselors help develop your attitude toward school and curriculum. A teacher, voluntarily or involuntarily, can use his or her position to manipulate your choice of courses, and a guidance counselor's recommendations influence your choice of postsecondary education, careers, and other future plans. In some cases these manipulations are done unconsciously, and even when teachers and guidance counselors consciously make gender-biased recommendations, they are sincere about the validity of their beliefs. Nevertheless, these outdated attitudes affect your education. The teachers you meet throughout your education shape your future.

Educators enforce gender biases in a number of ways. One way is through the use of gender-oriented classroom materials. These textbooks, school magazines, videos, posters, and multimedia resources often portray men as strong, independent, and powerful, while women are represented as weak, dependent, and subordinate. Role models play an important part in developing gender equality or gender bias. Educators are role models, but the school administration establishes stereotypical role models since more teachers are women and most principals are men.

Another way educators influence how you perceive your educational options is in the way they treat you. The interactions that occur in a classroom have a direct effect on how you feel about course work, your capabilities, your peers' capabilities, college, and career choices. Here are several examples of how this can work:

- A teacher's enthusiasm for history inspires you to be a history major in college.

- A teacher constantly states that physics is demanding and requires a strong mathematics background, causing you to abandon the physics course you were going to take as a senior.

- You want to become a doctor, but your art teacher tells you that you shouldn't because your artistic ability should be shared with society.

- Your reading teacher says that college is too hard for someone like you who has a learning disability.

These examples are actions that are obvious and would be hard to misinterpret, but teachers can create and reinforce gender bias in subtle ways too. These include additional attention and instruction given to male students, as well as the fact that in science and math courses, male students are called on to answer questions more often, their answers are taken more seriously, and they are allowed more access to computers and other scientific equipment. Also, female students may be treated condescendingly by teachers of some "unfeminine" subjects. All of these behaviors, blatant and subtle, contribute to a gender-biased educational environment and affect your education and that of your peers.

Physical Education and Gender Bias

Is your gym class coeducational? Most high schools today run coeducational gym classes. Does the presence of the opposite sex affect how you behave in gym class and the quality of your physical education? What do you think?

In many schools, female students either hate or love the school's top male athletes. One group of students may think these athletes are condescending, macho, and show-offs, whereas others think of these guys as strong, protective, and heroic. What happens when some of these "jocks" are in your gym class?

The girls who hate male athletes must prove their point. To do so, these women may act aggressively, are more competitive, and band together. This may defeat the purpose of holding coeducational physical education classes. Actions like these discourage the development of teamwork and foster gender bias by pitting females against males. Some physical education teachers "feed" these actions by making derogatory comments about female characteristics and "putting down" the male students who are not physical, have poor athletic ability, or, in the teacher's opinion, act too feminine. Comments that stress how women lack physical strength and athletic ability foster competition between genders and influence your judgment of the opposite sex.

Female students who see male athletes as attractive and heroic may perform poorly in gym class to attract attention. The actions of these students reinforce the gender-biased comments of the gym instructors. These women may have little confidence in their physical abilities, have low self-esteem, and be poor students. They may even believe—perhaps because of the gender biases they have learned from their parents or other authority figures—that they should find a man who will care for them rather than caring for themselves. Teenage girls who idolize athletes in this way reflect the classic stereotype of women as helpless and defenseless creatures. These females are often popular, pretty, and not interested in schoolwork. These girls embody the gender stereotype of what men supposedly look for in women, and correspondingly, the type of male students who look for these traits tend to treat women poorly—to view them as weak and easily dominated. Other teenage girls who do not embody the stereotype, and who are less pretty and less popular may become the butt of coarse sexual jokes, be ridiculed, and be continually harassed by the teenage boys who buy in to these outdated notions about women.

These gender bias attitudes influence how females treat

males outside of class too. The girls who have been harassed may become resentful. They may avoid the company of boys and thus fail to develop self-confidence around the opposite sex.

Teenage male athletes often believe that they must maintain the image of being the best sportsmen and competitors. In some cases, male athletes attempt to prevent women from joining their teams or participating in gender-specific sports. In a classroom environment this type of behavior causes increased competition and aggression, and stifles cooperation between the sexes. These teens show off for the opposite sex and sometimes, in doing so, embarrass themselves, which worsens the situation.

Many students, teachers, and school officials view male student athletes as school heroes. Athletes' teachers sometimes give them preferential treatment. Teachers who exhibit this type of behavior help validate gender stereotypes about athletic and physical abilities. This empowers athletes while making other students—male and female—self-conscious about their athletic deficiencies. Thus, the other students become victims of gender bias. Popular male athletes may harass, ridicule, and put-down the unattractive girls and "weaker" guys in their classes. These "macho" teens may abuse (physically and/or verbally) the male and female teens who behave differently, are "too feminine," or are too smart. They know they can do so because they are so highly valued by most of their peers and teachers.

Since schools take pride in the ability of their sports teams, athletes, especially male athletes, are a select and highly regarded portion of the student body. In most cases, coaches are also the school's physical education instructors, so gender bias and gender stereotyping become more obvious in gym classes. This type of environment influences all teens, affecting their behavior toward one another and their attitudes toward and opinions of the opposite sex.

When Teens Challenge

Some of you may have experienced gender-bias attitudes in school, and some of you may have challenged these attitudes. In some cases, you will not have any problem doing so. Sometimes, however, educators can use their authority to make life at school hard for students they decide are troublemakers. If you feel that any of your teachers or guidance counselors have created unreasonable situations, you should get your parents' support. You and your parents can address these issues with the principal and other school officials. Today gender bias is not generally tolerated by school administrators. By involving the administration you should be able to improve your situation.

If going to school officials does not help, be patient. Eventually you will be out of the problematic teacher's class. In the meantime, you should keep copies of your graded exams, papers, or any other course work. Doing this will give you an idea of what your grade should be and will serve as proof if the educator's bias influences your eventual grade unfairly. In addition, you can keep a daily journal of unusual events and, with permission, record class lectures. This will provide illustrations of the gender-biased environment.

In order to get the best education, you must be

assertive. Insist that you be treated fairly, enroll in the courses you want to take, choose the career that interests you, and continue your education the way you feel is best for you. You must make choices in life, and the best way is to learn and make educated choices. You will need guidance from your parents, family, teachers, and other adults whom you trust. But the final decision is yours. You are entitled to an education, and it is up to you to make it the best education possible.

Dating and Relationships

It's four o'clock, and Sarah is on the phone with Ray, her boyfriend. An hour quickly passes as the two talk about the kids in their school. Finally Sarah's mom calls upstairs and asks Sarah to get off the phone. Reluctantly, Sarah tells Ray she has to go and tells him she will call later.

After dinner Sarah calls Ray again. The two talk for half an hour. Sarah says good-bye and returns to her homework. With her homework complete, Sarah calls Ray a third time. In the middle of their conversation, Sarah hears strange clicking noises on the line. Then her mom gets on and tells her to get off the phone and stay off. Hesitantly, Sarah tells Ray she'll see him tomorrow at school.

Sarah goes into the living room and joins her family. Her brother looks at her, snickers, and makes a snide comment about how much time she spends on the phone. Sarah returns the glare and explains that when he has a girlfriend he'll spend just as much time on the phone.

Like Sarah, many of you have boyfriends or girlfriends. How much time do you spend on the phone? Who calls more often? Which of you, female or male, is more interested in the relationship?

Dating and relationships have changed. What was traditional for your parents' generation is old-fashioned to you and your peers. When your parents were dating, girls almost never called the boys. Now who calls the most? Usually, it is the girl.

Dating and Dating Etiquette

Some of you may not be allowed to date yet, but eventually, most of you will. In most cases your dating is done primarily by phone. You see your boyfriend or girlfriend in school, but outside of school, most of your time together is spent on the phone. Today, girls call guys, they ask the guys on dates, and they even ask guys to "go out." Going steady is what your parents called going out, and when they were dating, a girl would never even think of asking a guy to go steady.

Most teens know that it is hard to be popular without being involved in a relationship. But dating in today's society is complex. Morals and times have changed, and the physical aspects of a relationship tend to progress much faster. French kissing has become a regular part of dating, and for many teens, sex by the third date is not uncommon. Currently, many teens believe that losing their virginity is an indication of maturity and a requirement for a lasting relationship.

Male teens may view sex as just recreation or view girls as potential conquests, while females may view sex as an expression of love or just want to "get it over with." Some teens are pressured into moving the physical side of relationships forward by friends or even family, others by their background or circumstances. For example: Some female

46

teens have friends who want to hear "all the details." Some fathers give their teenage sons condoms as soon as they start to date. Then there are the teens who are athletes, cheerleaders, or members of other popular groups. These teens' peers often expect them to be sexually advanced and involved in "steamy" relationships. These circumstances and beliefs create expectations about the way teens should behave on a date. Dating etiquette varies with the situation, the common values in the area in which you live, and the current trends in society. There is no hard and fast set of rules to follow. Dating etiquette, especially about the physical aspects of the date, is between you and your date. No one should dictate your behavior or make you do something you are uncomfortable doing.

Today, it is just as appropriate and usual for the girl to ask a guy out as it is for the guy to ask a girl. Dates can be one-on-one or group events. A date may involve talking on the phone, meeting at the local hangout, going to the movies, or just chilling at each other's homes. Remember, what happens during the date should not be determined by your friends or what everyone else says they are doing. What happens during your date should be between you and your date. Both of you should be in agreement, and neither of you has the right to pressure the other into something he or she is uncomfortable doing. Dating should be an enjoyable experience.

Dating and Its Effect on Teen Boys

If you are a guy, do you feel that girls are pressuring you to date? Some of you may be very popular and have girls calling your homes all the time. How does that make you feel? At first, you may have felt pleased and proud that all these girls were after you. But perhaps after a while, all the phone calls did was to create more pressure and stress in your life. Maybe all this attention makes you feel self-conscious. If you have a girlfriend, you may have trouble finding time to spend with her, your other friends, your family, or time just for yourself.

Have you ever been the subject of gossip? Teens often compare their experiences. Friends discuss almost everything together. The girls that call you and that you are interested in will tell a friend, and sooner or later this information will get around. Some of what these girls discuss may be true, some may not; some might be exaggerations of the facts, and some may be accurate. It probably will bother you, and that is normal, but think about what you and your friends say about some of the girls in your classes. Don't you gossip with your friends, too? Aren't some of the discussions you have with your friends about girls—how certain girls look, dress, or act?

Do you and your friends pursue the girls you are interested in dating? Do your friends push you to date? Do they push you to pursue girls they think will "go all the way"? Do they push you to date a certain type of girl or one specific girl? No matter which aspect of dating you are dealing with, you will probably feel some pressure, stress, or frustration. It isn't any easier to be the pursuer than it is to be pursued.

When you are the pursuer, you may have to deal with rejection; not every teenage girl you meet will be interested in dating you. When this happens, do you and your friends start nasty gossip about the girl that "dumped" you? If you do, that would not be unusual. Guys, too, can spread some very nasty rumors about girls. That behavior is influenced by gender attitudes too. Sometimes, it may be your friends who make up the stories, because of their loyalty to you. But sometimes because you are hurt, you don't think of the consequences, the thought of revenge dulls the pain and you create the gossip.

You are not alone. Most teen boys have problems with dating and facing girls. There are various types of problems. Some boys are constantly nagged by girls who call all the time. Others chase girls and cannot get any of them to go out on a date. And some guys are just too busy or are not interested in dating yet. Whatever the circumstances, dating is not easy for anyone—male or female, young or old. Gender biases and expectations that are deeply rooted in our society can make dating complicated. Teens are not the only ones who do not always understand the opposite sex. As a teenager, you have to first understand what your needs, goals, and ambitions are without being influenced by your peers. Then you can relax and start to enjoy being with members of the opposite sex.

Dating's Effect on Teen Girls

For most girls, the reality in high school is that they have to date to be considered popular. You may be less likely to be invited to parties without a date. Once you have a date and he becomes a steady boyfriend, the situation can become even more complicated.

Today, there are several types of pressure and stress that

are brought on by dating and having a steady boyfriend. First, there is the question of whether your friends accept your choice of boyfriend. Do they think he is a good choice, or "bad news"? In some ways, either one can produce problems. If your friends approve, they may pressure you into getting emotionally or sexually involved with him more seriously than you want to. Sometimes this pressure comes from their own behavior—they may be sexually active and feel guilty, and believe that if you become sexually active too, it will make their choice more acceptable. Second, if your friends don't approve, they may pressure you to "dump" him. Sometimes friends may be more objective and notice behaviors that you do not, such as possessiveness and jealousy.

A boyfriend who is possessive and jealous creates hidden anxiety and stress. In that situation, your boyfriend may not allow you to spend much time with your friends. If you talk to a male friend, your boyfriend may become angry at or even violent toward him or at you. Your boyfriend may have his friends watching you constantly. This affects the amount of freedom and independence you can maintain. The situation can create more than just anxiety and stress; it can also cause suppressed fear and anger. Anger at the situation and anger at yourself for creating and not ending the situation. Also, a possessive boyfriend or ex-boyfriend who is angry may spread gossip about your sexual activities— true or untrue—throughout your school. Despite the changes in gender roles that have taken place in recent years, teenage girls are often still judged by their sexual "reputations." Girls who are sexually active may be viewed as "sluts," and girls who are not may be considered "prudes."

Another issue involved with dating is your assertiveness. Do you ask a guy you like if he is interested in you, and if so, when? Do you wait for him to make the first move, or do you make it? Some girls have their friends ask a guy if he is interested. Others may ask for themselves and some girls just wait for the guy to express his interest. Which way is correct? When is it proper to be assertive? Is it right for you to ask a guy out? How do you feel about it? Gender biases that you or your peers hold may lead you to believe that you should behave a certain way. But there are no right answers for everyone. These are all questions you must answer for yourself.

As you read earlier the "rules" of dating have evolved. What used to be taboo is now normal behavior. Sexual activities that were once reserved until marriage are now sometimes done on a first date. Society presents a very confusing picture regarding dating and sexuality, especially for young women. On one hand you may have been taught that sex is dangerous and sinful, but then you see a television show that describes sex as a character's one moment of true happiness. You are told that it is OK not to have a boyfriend but then you are ridiculed and labeled a loser if you do not.

How do these contradictions make you feel? You may be confused, anxious, hurt, resentful, or angry. No matter how you feel, none of these emotions is right or wrong. Dating isn't easy. Often, it is very stressful. Some girls will even tell you that they are afraid to go on dates. There is nothing wrong with feeling this way, or with any of the other feelings you may be experiencing. It is important that you do what is right for you and not succumb to peer pressure. Fear is a healthy response to relatively unknown situations. It makes you aware and cautious. Awareness and caution are good ways to respond to the stress and anxiety that accompanies dating. Whatever you decide to do, in the end, only you will have to face your feelings and the consequences of your actions.

The Date

Many of you have probably already gone on your first date. Did you know what to expect? A date can take many forms. You and your date may spend the time at one or the other's home. Your date may take place at the movies, the mall, a party, or the local hangout. Together, you may meet a group of friends and go somewhere with them or hang out at someone's house.

Usually, when dating involves a group, several people will chip in to pay for food and beverages or a video. But when you and your date do something special together, who pays? The answer to this question varies, but it may be determined in part by gender roles.

Traditionally, when a guy asked a girl out, he was responsible for all costs and transportation. Today, this is sometimes still true. Typically, for instance, when a couple goes to the prom, the boy will pay for everything. But there are also several other options, all of which depend on the circumstances surrounding the date. Examples include:

⮑ If one of you doesn't have enough money, you both may pay your own way, or the person who has more money will pay.

⮑ If the date is part of a special event, like a birthday, then the gift-giver will pay for everything.

⮑ To assert your independence and avoid feeling obligated to your date, you will pay for yourself.

Dating can be traditional or nontraditional. Today, society has different standards. Women are more independent and assertive. Most of the current trends in dating reflect these changes.

Same-Sex Friends and Gender Roles

Just about everyone has friends of the same sex. These are the friends you confide in and trust. During your childhood, these friendships were simple, but now that you are an adolescent, friendships with members of the same gender can become complicated.

If you are female, your other female friends may be dating or already have a steady boyfriend. You may have a close friend who has a boyfriend and no longer spends much time with you. When you are together, perhaps all your friend talks about is her boyfriend—what he's like, who his friends are, what she thinks of his friends, how he behaves, and sometimes even intimate details of what they have done on their dates. Your friend may have ideas of how you should behave in a relationship that are different from yours. This can cause tension between you.

Your friend may begin pressuring you to find a boyfriend. If you are already in a relationship, she may pressure you to become sexually active. This type of peer pressure may strain friendships and hurt feelings. Sometimes you may feel that your friend doesn't care about you or that she is too focused on her boyfriend. These feelings are not uncommon. But be patient and give both of these friendships—yours with her and her relationship—time. Strong friendships can usually survive change. If your ideas about appropriate behavior for teenage girls are too different, however, you may find your friendship coming to an end.

Same-sex friendships are accepted among females more easily than among males. Guys in today's society are discouraged from displaying affection toward others of their gender. Such behavior is viewed as effeminate and unmasculine. The closeness of male friendships often ends up being expressed in terms of discussions of sexual conquests and sporting events rather than more serious or intimate conversation. If male friends get too close or display too much affection, their reputations and masculinity are questioned. They may be ridiculed by their peers and, sometimes, even labeled as homosexuals.

Consequences like these make same-sex friendships among adolescent males a source of anxiety. At a time when close friendships are usually needed the most, they can become almost too risky to maintain.

For most of your life, your friends were probably of the same gender. Now, in your teens, along with all the other changes you are experiencing, society expects you to alter your views on friendship. Maintaining your established friendships while creating new friendships with members of the opposite sex can cause anxiety and stress. Friendships will be strained and sometimes broken. Relationships, whether they are with members of the same sex or the opposite sex, all require work from both parties. Good relationships need people to be considerate of each other. Good relationships need time, effort, and cooperation from both people. Dealing with friendships and dating is just one aspect— but a very important one—of teen life.

Gender Influences
on Social Activities

Victoria sat and listened while the band teacher played the different musical instruments. She knew he was demonstrating them because she and the other sixth-grade students had to decide which one they wanted to play, but so far, she didn't like what she heard. Victoria thought, "Guess I'm not going to learn to play a musical instrument." She let her mind wander.

In the middle of daydreaming, she suddenly sat attentively as the sound of the trombone sent tingles up her spine. Listening to the music, she decided, "That's it! That's the instrument I want to play." She signed up for trombone lessons right away.

Several months passed, and Victoria was doing well and enjoying her lessons. One afternoon, however, she was practicing and could not play a few of the notes. No matter how hard she tried the notes she blew were wrong.

The next day at her lesson she asked her teacher what she was doing wrong. To her surprise, it turned out that the problem was the length of her arms. The teacher explained that to hit those notes she had to move the trombone slide to a specific point, and apparently, that point was beyond her reach. He recommended that she switch to a different instrument.

Disappointed, Victoria went home and told her mom. After a brief discussion, Victoria decided to switch to the saxophone. But her mom was concerned that a saxophone hanging on her neck would be too heavy. She wanted Victoria to see how it felt before they made the final decision. Victoria's mom said she would come along when it was time for Victoria to tell the band teacher her decision.

Victoria and her mom met with the band teacher and explained the problem. To their surprise, the band teacher asked, "Why not play the clarinet? It's similar to the saxophone and much more feminine."

Victoria was annoyed and insulted. Her mom, surprised at the band teacher's response, looked at him and replied, "I don't care if the instrument is 'masculine' or 'feminine.' I just want Victoria to enjoy playing it.

"When I was young, my parents wouldn't let me play the trumpet because they thought it was too masculine. I ended up playing clarinet and hating it. Because of that experience, I don't play any musical instrument, can't remember how to read music, and don't enjoy listening to instrumental music. I don't want that to happen to my daughter."

The band teacher understood how her mom felt and agreed to let Victoria try on a saxophone. He gave Victoria a saxophone to try, then showed her how to attach it to the neck strap and how to hold it.

On the trip back home, Victoria told her mom that the saxophone was not too heavy. The next day, Victoria switched from the trombone to the saxophone. She has been playing it ever since.

Music and Gender

Do any of you play in a band—the school band, your own, or a friend's? Close your eyes and picture the members of the band. Notice the instrument each member of the band plays. Do any members of the band play instruments that are atypical for their gender? You may think this question is ridiculous. But think about it—how many female drummers have you seen?

Researchers have conducted studies to determine the gender associations of different musical instruments. One study asked undergraduate students to rate seventeen musical instruments. The results labeled the harp, flute, and piccolo with the highest feminine rating and the trumpet, string bass, and tuba with the highest masculine rating. Although this study was performed in 1981, another study in 1992 showed that gender association of certain instruments remains.

Does the gender association of an instrument affect you? If you play an instrument, how did you decide which one to play? A study carried out in 1993 asked 990 band students how they chose the instrument they play. This study revealed that the students' choices were influenced by:

➷ Any previous experience with musical instruments

➷ Family involvement as they decided on their choice

➷ The gender associated with the instrument

Why are there genders associated with musical instruments? Most of these associations began because of a variety of stereotypes about physical ability and appropriate behavior for women. In the past, male musicians did not believe that women were physically capable of playing certain instruments well. Some instruments, such as brass instruments, were thought to be too masculine for women to play. Consider the two statements below.

> *"If more girl drummers had cradle-rocking experiences before their musical endeavors, they might come closer to getting on the beat."*
> (Downbeat *magazine, 1938)*

> *How Can You Play a Horn with a Brassiere?*
> *(Headline in* Downbeat *magazine, 1938)*

Do these quotes suggest that certain musical instruments were considered too difficult for women?

Historically, women musicians have been underrepresented or ignored in textbooks. In addition, although upper-class women usually learned a musical instrument as part of their education, they were forbidden to play in public until the twentieth century in some parts of Western society. Since female musicians had little public exposure, most men did not recognize women as competent musicians. Also, "proper" women did not play in orchestras or bands. Times change, fortunately, and in 1888 Caroline B. Nichols founded a women's orchestra. By the end of the century, there were thirty all-female orchestras in the United States.

During the 1930s, as a public relations gimmick, male producers and promoters put together all-women bands.

Despite their origins as gimmicks, some of these bands produced excellent musicians and were popular until the end of World War II when jazz became the dominant type of music. Female bands and orchestras helped change or eliminate some of the gender association of musical instruments. But as the studies that you read about earlier illustrate, students still associate specific instruments with certain genders. How does this affect you? If you don't play a musical instrument and have no intention of starting, the gender association of musical instruments may not have an effect on you.

But what about your friends who do play instruments? Did you or anyone else comment on their choice of instrument? It is possible that you, unknowingly, demonstrated your particular gender association with one or more musical instruments. Maybe you made a statement about the type of person who typically plays that instrument. Or you might have commented on and named some famous people who play that type of instrument.

You are not the only one who influences your friends. Instrumental music teachers play a big part in a choice of instrument. First, band teachers are more likely to be male than female, so as a teenage girl playing an instrument, you may not have a role model available. Also, most schools usually offer lessons in specific instruments because these are the instruments the instructor is qualified to teach. In some cases band teachers have specific feelings about whether males or females are more capable of learning a particular type of instrument. Teachers who feel this way may strongly influence a student's instrument choice. Sometimes school administrators have to try to meet state or Board of Education requirements for minority participation in school activities, and this may also influence the suggestions they make to students.

In addition, your friend's parents may influence her choice of musical instrument. Unlike Victoria, some teens have parents who believe that certain instruments are not feminine or proper for females to play. Some parents push their child to learn an instrument the parent always wanted to learn. And sometimes, as in Victoria's case, parents will let their child choose an instrument on their own. Lastly, the instrument that you or your friends choose may be based on previous experience. A musical instrument that you have already begun to learn may be the one you choose to continue studying in high school. Or you may choose to change instruments, either because you want to learn another one or you dislike the first instrument.

Once you or your friend have chosen a musical instrument, is it accepted? Do females who choose a "masculine" instrument become the target of snide remarks? Do males who choose a "feminine" instrument have to defend their masculinity? The answers to these questions vary. Would you pick on someone because of the musical instrument he or she plays? Some people have been raised with strong gender stereotypes. These teens would criticize and ridicule. Other teens have a more accepting background, and the type of instrument that someone plays would not affect how they treat that person. Similar statements are true about teachers and parents. People vary, and so will reactions to different sexes playing certain musical instruments.

Sometimes these reactions can be vicious or just plain mean. There is not much you or your peers can do about this behavior from other people. You may not be able to change another person's beliefs. Gender stereotyping is the result of many influences over a period of years. Fortunately, gender differences affecting a student's choice of musical instrument have lessened over the years, and educators continue to work at creating gender equality in music education.

Dance and Gender

When you go to a club or a party, there are usually some people dancing. They may be dancing in a line or group, or as couples. Teens dance at these social events and don't think twice about gender issues. But did you know that during a certain time in history, disreputable women were the only females who danced?

Native American, Latino, and other cultures have traditionally incorporated dance as part of their religious and social life. But white culture in the United States has only a limited tradition of social dancing and almost no theatrical dancing. The strict Puritan culture, which frowned on music and dance for pleasure, dominated the late eighteenth and early nineteenth centuries. Women who danced showed their legs, and therefore dancers were labeled disreputable and dancing was considered taboo. Dancing eventually became an acceptable social activity. Ideas about dance were modified drastically. Not only did dance become acceptable, it also became one of the few social activities not dominated by men. Today, gender issues involving dance focus on encouraging male participation.

When you go to a club, party, or school dance, there are always guys dancing. But what about boys and men taking dance classes? Anyone who has taken a dance class whether it is jazz, tap, ballet, or hip-hop has noticed that there are usually very few guys present. Social dancing is an acceptable activity for either gender, but males who choose to participate in dance education programs experience gender bias.

Society has a definite opinion about male and female dancers. Certain styles of dance are acceptable for men to practice. Jazz dance is one example; there are many famous male jazz dancers. On the other hand, ballet is gender-stereotyped as feminine. There are only a few famous male ballet dancers, and when most people see a male ballet dancer, they are likely to assume he is homosexual. Society, when it accepts the male dancer, requires that his dance moves be more strenuous and powerful than a woman dancer's. Even with these physical demands met, male dancers are often ridiculed and their sexuality questioned.

Does this happen with female dancers? Dance is associated with femininity. Women participate in recreational, educational, and professional dance. Their participation is accepted and condoned by society. Their femininity is not questioned, and they are not taunted.

Presently, male students are the minority in dance education. They are on the receiving end of gender bias, and it is the male dance student who will benefit from reform in dance education. Educators are attempting to improve male participation in dance education and eliminate or reduce gender bias in dance.

Sports and Gender

Does your school have teams in these sports?

- Soccer

- Softball

- Basketball

- Swimming

- Football

- Ice hockey

- Tennis

- Baseball

- Indoor and outdoor track and field

- Wrestling

- Field hockey

- Gymnastics

All of these team sports may exist in your school. Reread the list, and as you do, think about your school teams. Are there male and female teams for each of these sports? Are there coed teams for any of them?

When you reread the list of sports, did you find that some, such as soccer, track and field, swimming, gymnastics, basketball, and tennis are activities in which both women and men participate? Do some sports have different names and rules for the male team than for the female team? Examples are baseball and ice hockey (usually played by boys) versus softball and field hockey (usually played by girls). Did you notice any all-male sports, such as wrestling and football? Why do you think that participation in these sports is limited to men? Are there any sports at your school that girls play and guys do not?

Women have always had to fight to be allowed to participate in sports. Historically, women's gym classes were designed to keep women healthy, improve their looks, or prepare their bodies for giving birth. From 1890–1920, this changed somewhat. Women began playing college baseball around that time. Then in the 1920s, because the public felt American women were becoming too "masculine," schools and colleges ended their women's sports programs. It was not until the passing of Title IX in 1972 that women's sporting competitions returned. Title IX, one of the Educational Amendments passed by the U.S. Congress, states the following: "Any educational program or activity that receives federal aid cannot exclude people from participation based on their sex."

Because of this educational amendment, sports programs and professional degree programs were opened to women. Title IX gave schools the flexibility to establish programs based on student body interest. Thus, for example, if there were not enough women interested in participating in football or wrestling, schools were not required to set up those programs.

Today, most schools offer a variety of competitive sports. In almost all cases, sports teams are not coed. The majority of the time, the reason for this is based on gender stereotypes about physical strength. Coeducational football and hockey teams do not exist, for example, because women are not believed to be strong enough to compete against men in those sports. A few women students have challenged these all-male teams and demanded that they be allowed to join them. In doing so, they have had to deal with unfavorable publicity, peer pressure, and in most cases, little support from their school administrators. Unfortunately, often once a female player does successfully join an all-male team, the ridicule, aggression of the male players, and the pressure to "show the world" is too great for her to handle, and she leaves the team.

Today, most sports are represented by both sexes. There are women wrestlers, women track and field athletes, and both male and female gymnasts, figure skaters, and golfers. Segregation in two of the most physically demanding sports, ice hockey and football, still exists and will probably remain for some time. Although government and society made great strides during the twentieth century in decreasing sexual discrimination, there are still some "no-woman's-lands." Until enough women demand to become a part of these male-dominated sports, gender bias in these events will continue.

Whether or not you realize it, the gender bias exhibited in professional sports has had an impact on your life. If you have watched professional sports as you have grown up, this has influenced your expectations about your athletic ability in specific sports. Because you were almost certainly exposed to gender-biased sporting events, the sports you choose to play are influenced by your own gender and preconceptions about it. Few women make wrestling their choice of team sport, but your school's gymnastics team is probably all female. At the same time, most men prefer basketball, baseball, football, and hockey to gymnastics, tennis, or other sports that seem less "masculine."

Another more subtle way that your gender influences your choice of sport is how the media treats female athletes. The media typically oversimplifies the importance of women's sports by under-reporting female athletic accomplishments and women's sporting events while giving far more attention to men's sports. These subtle "put-downs" of the type of sports chosen by women indirectly influence which sports males choose to play. By sending messages that women's sports are unimportant and undemanding, the media influences what the male population believes are masculine sporting activities.

You and your friends are just starting to become independent and conscious of your own personalities and selves. At a time in your life when so much change is taking place, you feel that you need the security that peer friendships provide. The influence of your peers, the media's subtle categorizing of sporting activities, and your own gender stereotyping (both conscious and unconscious) have an effect on how you picked the sport you play and help determine the social activities you participate in.

Sports and social activities are an important part of

adolescence. Understanding how your gender influences the choices you make will help reduce gender stereotyping. Change occurs gradually, and only when people are willing to understand and modify their beliefs. Developing gender equity in social activities by reducing the influence that gender has on these activities begins with your awareness that gender bias exists. Once you and your friends understand the how and the why, then change is possible.

The Effect of Appearance on Gender Roles

Terry glanced at the clock and thought, "Oh, no. I've spent over twenty minutes trying on different outfits. Soon I'm going to hear Mom yelling about the time."

Like clockwork, Terry's mother shouted up the stairs, "Terry, you've been dressing forever! If you don't hurry, you'll miss the bus!"

Terry glanced in the mirror and changed for the fifth time. Terry checked each item of clothing for brand-name labels and that certain fit. Terry knew that the "in group" would be sure to notice if both were not right. Finally satisfied, Terry ran downstairs to eat and catch the school bus.

What you wear and how you look are important. For most of your life, you have heard how important it is to make a good first impression. Your appearance is one of the first things people notice. The way you look influences what these people believe about your social and educational background, as well as what they believe you are capable or incapable of achieving.

You may think that this is an exaggeration, but it is not. Consider what you wore or will wear to your first job interview. Do you dress the same way to play ball, go to a club or party, or go to school? Probably not. When you dress for these activities, you are very conscious and careful about what you wear. This is not an accident. How you were raised and what you were taught by your immediate and extended family help you understand that different occasions call for different styles of dress. Therefore, you dress certain ways to maintain the appearance required for that occasion or circumstance. The way you dress for various occasions and events reflects the impact appearance has on your behavior and social status. Appearance has an effect on all our lives. Does appearance also affect gender roles?

Time brings changes to this as well as other social issues. Women and men have been expected to dress in specific ways for much of history. In Puritan times, a woman's legs could not be bare. During the Victorian era, women wore clothing that exaggerated their rear ends, with corsets that forced an unrealistically small waist. Women during Victorian times wore clothes that enhanced femininity, while men dressed in a manner that accentuated masculinity. Women wore dresses or skirts, men wore pants. These standards remained for years. It wasn't until the late sixties that girls were allowed to wear pants in school.

Times have changed. Today, most schools do not have a gender-based dress code. In some religious schools, the female uniform still consists of a skirt and blouse, and girls may not wear pants to school. But at most other schools, the rules are less strict. At work, men and women wear suits, and some women even wear ties. Everyone wears jeans. Males and females can have long or short hair, wear earrings and other jewelry, and wear clothes that are considered unisex in both color and style.

Today, acceptable appearance is often determined by the brand names you buy and wear rather than whether you wear a skirt or pants. However, even with the acceptance of "male" styles being worn by women, appearance still has a tremendous effect on gender roles. Appearance determines how easily you are accepted by the popular group, your ability to obtain a date, and even your capacity to make friends. Females, in particular, have tremendous pressure placed on them because of appearance. Adolescent girls may experience depression if they can't be thin enough, pretty enough, or dress well enough to be popular with guys. Teen guys aren't exempt from the gender-role effects of appearance, either. Today, many guys are as style- and clothes-conscious as women. Specific brands can label you cool or a "geek." And young women will choose boyfriends based on physical appearance. Adolescent males not only must dress the part, but they must be "buff." Appearance not only affects gender roles but in some cases, also reinforces them.

Cross-Dressing

What about adolescents who dress flamboyantly or in clothing usually worn by the opposite sex? Do you know guys who dress and act feminine or girls who dress and act masculine? In some cases, what these teens are wearing is acceptable by today's standards. Both men and women may choose to pierce their ears. At one time, depending on which ear was pierced, a man with an earring might have been labeled as a homosexual. In most parts of the country now, however, earrings worn by men are acceptable, and currently many men who pierce their ears, pierce both ears. In addition to earrings, some male teens wear necklaces, bracelets, and rings. Jewelry, once thought of as a feminine accessory, is now acceptable for both sexes.

However, there are limits. Male teens who wear makeup or dress and act "too" feminine are labeled as homosexuals. Adolescent and adult males who flaunt an overly feminine appearance challenge the standard male gender role model and create a situation that some find threatening. Teens, especially teen boys, who feel threatened by this challenge often respond with cruelty, aggression, and sometimes violence.

Girls who dress and act too masculine have similar problems, for the same reasons. These girls are labeled as lesbians and face the same treatment as their male counterparts. Even today, with all the changes in our thinking about gender roles, any stray from the "norm" brings criticism, ridicule, and shame.

What If You Don't Look Your Role?

Teens are influenced by their parents, other family members, teachers, friends, and peers. They are also influenced by society and cultural expectations. These expectations can encompass many areas including appearance. What happens when teens do not match the appearance society has created for their gender?

Even today, a teen's gender is associated with a predetermined appearance. You read about these "appearance roles" earlier. Adolescent females are expected to be pretty, but not too pretty, be thin but still feminine and not sticklike, and have a clear complexion. Adolescent males are expected to have good skin, be well-built, and appear clean-cut. What happens to teens who cannot meet these expectations? What conditions do these teens have to face? How do they cope?

Teens who don't look their role face a variety of situations. The majority, both male and female, have few friends and do not date or socialize much with their peers. Female teens dwell on their appearance. If they are not satisfied with their looks, they may experience depression. Some resort to drastic dieting measures and develop eating disorders that can be life-threatening. These girls also experience severe criticism and ridicule from their peers. In some cases, the behavior of their peers forces these teens to react aggressively. In other cases, these girls just retreat into their own world, becoming distant and isolated.

Male adolescents have similar problems. If a male teen's appearance does not match the current trends, they, too, may have difficulty maintaining peer friendships and getting dates. When teen guys do not have the appearance expected for their gender, they have to deal with put-downs and mocking, just as teen girls do. Guys who deal with these situations react, many times, by becoming aggressive and creating trouble. By doing so, they receive the attention, even if it is negative, that they desire from their peers.

Appearance affects both sexes' gender roles. However, female gender roles are affected much more than male roles. The female body is still treated as a sexual object in our society. Women are not considered truly equal by many male and female members of society, and the old female stereotypes, although more subtle, are still present. Women and adolescent girls are expected to look a certain way. Society teaches girls to be thin and beautiful. Magazines preach that girls should diet and exercise to attract boys. These constant reminders of the importance of their looks increase the effect that appearance has on female gender roles. This pressure placed on adolescent girls makes them feel that appearance controls their social life.

As you read in the beginning of this chapter, times change. Women still experience the most pressure from society to maintain a specific "look." But even men are starting to become very self-conscious about their appearance. Teens of both sexes have always been very aware of how their bodies changed during adolescence. Now, with all the pressure society places on a person's looks, adult men are becoming concerned with their appearance as well. Radio stations feature advertisements by plastic surgeons that are designed to attract males and females. Designers now create high fashions for men and women. And cosmetics companies have lines of skin-care products and perfumes formulated for men and women. These advertisements for clothing and cosmetic products are not restricted to adults. They are also aimed at teens. Through advertising, these companies create the sense that appearance is (or should be) extremely important in your life. Then the companies depend on your need to maintain your looks so that you will keep buying their products. Appearance is big business.

Your appearance is important to you. It affects your sense of gender identity (how masculine or feminine you feel) and determines how you feel about yourself. At a time when acceptance by your peers means everything to you, you may really believe that appearance controls your life. Keep in mind that what is considered "in" now, will be "out" six months or a year from now. What may not look good on you now may look great in six months. No one "look" lasts forever, changes in appearance occur gradually after a lot of effort and work, and looks aren't as important in adulthood as they are when you are a teen. These statements may be difficult to accept when you are dealing with the present. Just keep in mind that change always happens, and be patient—your turn will come. It may take a lot of work or time, but eventually you will come to terms with your appearance and be happy with yourself.

How the Media
Influences Gender Roles

Madelynn walked into her living room, tossed her books onto the couch, picked up the remote, and turned on the television. Tuning in to an afternoon talk show, she sat down to watch. Madelynn watched as guest women and teens came on stage in tight skirts and very small tops. The females each in turn strutted across stage wiggling their hips and rear ends. As they walked, they yelled, "If you've got it, flaunt it, and I've got it." The audience, both males and females, screamed and whooped, cheering them on and supporting their conduct.

After everyone was seated and the studio audience quieted down, the talk show host introduced the guests and explained how each guest brought some-one they cared about who desperately needed a makeover.

Madelynn watched as each guest introduced their friends. She noticed that all the friends were dressed in comfortable clothing, mostly pants and shirts. Nothing each guest wore was revealing or very fem-inine. Madelynn continued to watch because she liked to see how the makeovers turned out.

Finally, each of the guests' friends completed their make-overs. One at a time each came out on stage. While each person walked across stage displaying their new look they received "wolf whistles" and loud shouts of approval from the studio audience.

Madelynn noticed that all the women were now dressed in tight skirts and blouses or dresses. Madelynn thought, "Yuck, dressing that way isn't comfortable, especially for running between classes." She grabbed the remote in disgust, turned off the television and picked up the phone to call her friend.

Like Madelynn, you probably come home from school and watch television. Some of you may watch talk shows, animated cartoons, soap operas, game shows, or music shows. But did you ever stop to think about the effects these shows have on your life?

You've heard on news shows that television and movies influence teens and children. News programs report about the effects of television and movie violence. In this chapter, you will read how television, movies and other forms of media influence your gender role development.

Madelynn watched guests on a talk show, after having a makeover, come out dressed in tight skirts and blouses or tight dresses. Madelynn related the situation to her own circumstances and decided the outfits would not work in her situation. This was not the reaction that the producers of the television show expected or wanted. The producers may have sexually stereotyped women unconsciously. By giving all of these women this type of clothing, the producers, unknowingly, were reinforcing part of the female stereotype.

Male and Female Role Stereotypes

What are the typical male and female gender stereotypes? You probably already know these typical gender roles. At one time or another, you've heard or read the following verse:

> *Snips and snails, and puppy dogs' tails*
> *That's what little boys are made of.*
> *Sugar and spice, and everything nice*   P.P.G.
> *That's what little girls are made of.*

What does this verse tell you? It illustrates the fact that there are differences between the genders. It also seems to imply that girls and boys are opposites.

There are specific character traits associated with males and different traits associated with females. These traits create and represent typical male and female stereotypes. As you read earlier, from the time a child is born, society labels that child a specific sex. This is achieved in many ways, including the assignment of acceptable male/female colors, expectations of appropriate male/female behaviors, offering educational choices specific to gender, and presenting male/female stereotypical careers and sports.

The stereotypes associated with masculinity are:

↪ Activity

↪ Aggression

↪ Leadership

78

⇒ Independence

⇒ Roughness

⇒ Strength

Characteristics stereotypically representative of femininity are:

⇒ Inactivity

⇒ Passiveness

⇒ Dependence

⇒ Softness

⇒ Gentleness

⇒ Weakness

Stereotypes are generated about race, religion, careers, and gender. All stereotypes have an effect on people's lives. The above male/female characteristics have been instilled in your subconscious since the day you were born. The behaviors you know and believe to be correct for your gender influence your daily life and almost every activity you perform. Male/female stereotypes affect how you are treated by your parents, peers, educators, and society.

As you know, stereotypical gender roles are being challenged. The Equal Rights Amendment and Title IX have increased the number of women in the workforce, atypical higher education curriculums, and in sports. Today's culture is full of examples of some of the changes gender role stereotypes are undergoing. But change is slow and is often hindered. The media—television, movies, magazines, and commercials—has become the most popular means of communicating ideas to a large mass of people. Perhaps more than any other source, it is the media that changes, maintains, and educates people about today's definition of gender roles.

Cultural Influences on the Media's Use of Gender Roles

In 1985, author Neil Postman referred to television as a curriculum, saying that it is an information system designed to influence, teach, train, or civilize the intellect and character of children and adolescents. Through television, children and teens learn about gender roles, expectations, and information about their world.

Television, movies, and music videos are watched by adolescents more than ever before. Studies show that the average child and teen each watch about four hours of television per day. As our culture modifies the definition of gender roles, the media tries to modernize its concepts too.

Today, TV portrayals of mothers reflect the fact that women work and raise children. Television shows and commercials show female stars in roles equal in stature to male stars. Men and women are portrayed in occupations that are atypical for their gender. Men are even shown as single parents, raising children alone. But even with all these advances, the media is still behind the times in its portrayal of women. In a study reported in the April 1998 issue of *Shape* magazine, researchers analyzed twenty-five highly rated television programs, fifteen movies, three weeks' worth of top 20 music videos, and four issues of leading teen magazines. The following are some of the study's findings:

In movies:

 Females are shown working only half as often as males.

⇀ Females receive comments about their appearance twice as often as males.

On television:

⇀ Only 16 percent of men are thin or very thin.

⇀ In contrast, nearly half of the women are shown thin or very thin.

 Sixty-three percent of all television ads that target women were for appearance-related products.

⇀ Only 9 percent of television ads for appearance-related products are aimed at males.

These statistics demonstrate how our changing culture has influenced the way the media conveys gender roles. They also show that our culture has not yet reached gender equality. Part of the female stereotype has always focused on looks. Today, standards of beauty have changed, but the new standards are even harder for the average female to achieve. For example: In 1951 Miss Sweden was 5' 7" tall and weighed 151 pounds; while 1983's Miss Sweden was 5' 9" and weighed only 109 pounds. Tall and very thin has become a major part of the definition of feminine beauty.

Today, men may choose to stay home and raise the children. But the media's portrayal of important life choices like this is, in most cases, represented as comical, with scenes in which the stay-at-home dad bumbles and botches all or most of his parenting "jobs." This representation demeans the attempt to illustrate that men, too, can be competent caregivers and nurturing parents.

Our culture is changing, and many people are making attempts to create gender equality. These changes are most easily demonstrated by the media's representation of male and female gender roles. However, the media also illustrates that gender equality has not yet been achieved, and much work remains to be done before it is.

The Media's Effect on Teen Views of Gender Roles

You read earlier that the average teen watches about four hours of television a day. You also read that television has taken on a major teaching role in children's and adolescents' lives. A five-year study performed by the American Psychological Association discovered that watching television led to antisocial behavior, bad grades in school, and gender stereotyping. Perhaps surprisingly, the most influential component of television, and other forms of media, are the ads.

Watching four hours of television each day exposes you to over 120 commercials. And it has been proven that commercials have more of an effect on your view of gender roles than do television shows, movies, the music you listen to, music videos you watch, or the magazines you read. These concepts are illustrated by a 1985 study that suggested that television and its commercials have more influence on your gender role development and future aspirations than your parents, family, and educators. The only greater influence is that of your friends and peers.

How do commercials affect you? In several ways, television is a source that teens and children use to determine what is appropriate for their sex. It illustrates what teens and children may expect for their future and influences how you feel about yourself and others. How do these commercials do this? Consider the following:

- Male actors portray the doctors and scientists that give product endorsements.

- Voice-overs that have authority tend to be male.

- Women in commercials usually speak to babies, children, pets, women dieters, or someone in an inferior position.

- Female voices were used in commercials for dolls, accessories, stuffed animals, and feminine hygiene, headache, and dieting products.

- Commercials aimed at males have more action, scene changes, sound effects, and foreground music.

83

➷ On the other hand, commercials aimed at females have more conversations, background music, slow gradual scene changes, and images that portray softness and gentleness.

➷ In toy commercials, boys are shown with vehicles and building equipment, playing with construction sets and math- and science-based toys, and building models.

➷ In contrast, female toy commercials show dolls, housekeeping equipment, and beauty product toys.

The effect these commercials have may surprise you. As a child, you were exposed to these toy commercials. Almost all the toys that develop mathematical, manipulation, and spatial skills are aimed at males, and toys that develop nurturing qualities are aimed at females. These toys are designed to teach specific skills, and this illustrates how toys are made gender-specific.

The combination of all aspects of commercials tends to reinforce gender stereotypes. This is proven by a study performed in 1984 that concluded that viewers who watch the most television adhere to stereotypical gender roles and see themselves in careers typical for their gender. These findings were verified in a recent study done by a Western Connecticut State University student. This study also found that female roles in commercials are widening. Females have an increasing variety of roles available to them in occupations, family choices, and competitive sports. Although the study shows that the media's representation of gender roles is changing, the stereotypical male/female roles are still the ones most frequently portrayed.

Because the media presents these gender stereotypes and because today's culture is so closely tied to the media; it is important that you explore all of the possibilities that are available beyond the stereotypes associated with your sex. This is especially true since you live in a time in which the most opportunities are open to both males and females, whether it is to continue their education, select atypical careers, or be stay-at-home parents.

Changing Gender Roles in the Workplace

Melody's friends were always surprised to find out that her brother was thirteen years older than they were. Mel talked about him constantly, but they never realized that he was married.

All her life Melody looked up to her older brother. She remembered how he practically raised her while her parents were at work. How he helped her with her homework, taught her to play ball, and waited for her to come back from her first date. But her best memories of their times together were when she would help him work on his car. Watching her brother transform a "piece of junk" into a hot sports car was almost like watching a miracle take place. It was the thrill of converting a lifeless hunk of metal into a purring piece of machinery that convinced Melody what she wanted to do for a living. Melody wanted to be an automotive engineer.

Mel knew that engineering required a lot of time and education. But she also knew that she wanted to start working on cars sooner rather than later, so she decided to take some courses in auto mechanics as senior electives. Mel told her parents her plans and they were pleased, but surprised.

Today, Mel was taking her signed course selections to her guidance counselor. She arrived at the guidance office early, hoping her counselor would tell her whether her class choices were available. She waited anxiously as her counselor reviewed her form and checked each class's status on the computer. Suddenly, the counselor turned to Mel and said, "You must have made a mistake. According to your selection form, you signed up for auto mechanics. That can't be right."

Mel smiled and replied, "It's no mistake. I want to take that course."

Her guidance counselor looked at her in shock and answered, "I don't recommend it. It isn't the right course for you."

Thinking that the guidance counselor was behind the times, Mel said, "I know what is involved in this course. My parents approved my choice. Please just sign me up for the class."

Reluctantly, the guidance counselor agreed, and Mel got her auto mechanics course.

Have you ever had a similar discussion with your guidance counselor? Some of you may have. Today, high schools offer a wide variety of elective courses. Some of these courses seem to be designed for a specific gender. For example, food science and quilting are typically thought of as courses females would take, whereas scaled aviation design and auto mechanics would have a predominantly male student body. If gender equality truly existed in schools, a guidance counselor would not comment on course choices that were atypical for your gender.

However, as Mel found out and as studies have shown, guidance counselors tend to recommend courses and careers that are gender-typical.

How Gender Influences Career Choices

As you now know, your gender has a great deal of an effect on your life, especially when it comes to your choice of careers. You have probably begun to think about career choices, and some of you may already know which career you want to pursue. You may not have made a final decision about your choice of career. But all of you know that at some point in your life, you will have to work for a living.

Read this list of careers, carefully. While you read, picture someone doing that job.

⇨ Secretary

⇨ Librarian

⇨ Postal clerk

⇨ Physician's assistant

⇨ Firefighter

⇨ Engineer

⇨ Bank teller

⇨ Psychologist

⇨ Sales clerk

☞ Dentist

☞ Pharmacist

☞ Police detective

☞ Physician

☞ Architect

☞ Mail carrier

☞ Private child care worker

☞ Office clerk

☞ Lawyer

☞ Registered nurse

☞ Auto mechanic

Now, reread the above list and think about your mental image. What gender was the person you pictured in each occupation? The 1994 statistics shown below represent the percentage of women and men in that occupation.

	Women	Men
Secretary:	99%	1%
Librarian:	84%	16%
Postal clerk:	44%	56%
Physician's assistant	54%	46%
Firefighter:	2%	98%
Engineer:	8%	92%

Bank teller:	90%	10%
Psychologist:	59%	41%
Sales clerk:	49%	51%
Dentist:	13%	87%
Pharmacist:	38%	62%
Police detective:	11%	89%
Physician:	22%	78%
Architect:	17%	83%
Mail carrier:	34%	66%
Private child care worker:	97%	3%
Office clerk:	80%	20%
Lawyer:	25%	75%
Registered nurse:	94%	6%
Auto mechanic:	2%	98%

Was the person you pictured the one associated with the larger number? If so, you just experienced career gender bias. Our society not only exhibits this form of gender bias but teaches it too.

When you reviewed the career statistics, you noticed that most of the higher paying and more prestigious careers are dominated by men. Why? In the past, the man was head of the household, divorce was uncommon, and single women did not usually have children. During that period, women stayed home, raised children, prepared the meals, and kept house. Women and children were supported by the "man of the house." Because of this belief, women were thought of primarily as wives and mothers and were not considered legitimate workers. Therefore, women did not need good jobs with high pay. Men, however, had to work at jobs that provided wages large enough to support their families. These cultural expectations placed on men reinforced and perpetuated the male dominance of higher-paying careers.

The concept that men required higher pay created the gender bias you still see in careers today. In addition to linking income to gender in careers, society also tends to associate the skills, competencies, strengths, and other required job qualities with specific feminine and masculine traits. Here is one example: In 1970, because of the economic recession that was in effect then, men who had sold residential real estate left that job market to sell commercial real estate, which is usually more lucrative than residential. The jobs vacated by these men were filled by women. Employers argued that since women ran homes and knew their neighborhoods and schools they were "naturals" for this type of work.

Employers are not the only people who link job requirements to feminine and masculine traits. People in nontraditional occupations tend to maintain gender-typing by describing their work in gender-specific terms. For instance, a policewoman may view her work as social work, helping the community, whereas a male nurse might emphasize the physical strength and use of technology required to perform his job.

The fact that gender-typing remains is a sign of people's uneasiness with how others view their choice of careers. Although nontraditional career choices are becoming more common, they are still unusual enough that people will question the femininity or masculinity of persons in that career. Men in traditionally feminine careers are often thought of as less masculine, and sometimes even

considered to be homosexuals. Women in careers typically dominated by men are usually considered aggressive, not family-oriented, and unsympathetic—all traits
that indicate a lack of femininity.

Workers in gender-dominated fields usually find it difficult to accept the opposite gender into their occupation.
Sometimes these situations lead to sexual harassment,
aggression, and an uncomfortable work environment. The
work environment has been forced to undergo change,
however. Women and men are being accepted into atypical careers, and employers are finally realizing that these
employees are as valuable as those who are the "correct"
gender for their occupation.

Changes Occurring in the Work Environment

Society does not accept change easily. For years, employers benefited from the poor work conditions and low
wages they forced on employees who were not typical
candidates for that particular occupation. But in 1963 and
1964, two pieces of legislation forced major changes in
the work environment: the Equal Pay Act of 1963 and the
United States Civil Rights Act of 1964.

The Equal Pay Act of 1963 required that the private
work sector provided equal pay for equal work, meaning
that no two people with the same job description and
experience could be paid unequal salaries. The concept
of equal pay for equal work had already been granted to
federal civil service employees in 1923, but the Equal
Pay Act extended that right to all employees in the
United States.

The Civil Rights Act of 1964 made it illegal for employers to discriminate on the basis of sex when hiring, training, promoting, determining wages, or providing benefits or any other work condition. Amendments to this act provided protection against sexual harassment, enforced equal pay for equal value, and established affirmative action.

Prior to these pieces of legislation, in 1940 and 1960, women only made up 24 percent and 33 percent, respectively, of the total workforce. After the Civil Rights Act was enacted, however, the total percentage of women in the U.S. workforce increased. It has continued to increase; in 1980, women made up 43 percent, but by 1995, that number had risen to 46 percent.

The work environment has experienced other gender-related changes. Differences in gender affect working conditions, treatment of employees, work facilities, and relationships between coworkers.

An important aspect of the work environment is socializing, the development of a network of peers who will support and aid you in career development. Associating with coworkers provides a means to improve career positions, meet upper-management-level employees, and develop good working relationships. This important function of socialization is difficult in some cases, in part because of society's gender bias. For instance, in high-paying jobs, men and women must develop working relationships in order to improve their careers. But research shows that women physicians will usually associate with women medical students, interns, and residents instead of either female nurses or male doctors. The women doctors need to maintain good working relationships with the female nurses but cannot get too friendly. Becoming too close would lower the female physicians' status because nursing is considered an occupation with a lower standing. Women physicians need to develop relationships with their colleagues, but male physicians may not treat them as equals. On the other hand, male nurses have no trouble associating with male doctors. And this association benefits them by affirming their masculinity, allowing them to relate to a group with higher status, and earn good performance reviews.

Men of lower social status and women have always been viewed differently by society—in the work environment as well as in general. But legislation and better access to training and education have improved working conditions and opportunities.

Some of you may have parents or other family members who have experienced discrimination on the jobs. In some cases, the problem was probably mentioned to a supervisor and then resolved, but in other cases, it may not have improved. Your parent or other family member may have found new work because of an unresolved discrimination issue at a previous job. How did you feel when you learned of these problems and how they were resolved?

Many of you may already be working. You may have a job in a fast-food store, restaurant, supermarket, or department store. For some, these jobs are not indicative of your career goals but are "in-between" jobs—jobs that help you prepare for a career, allow you to experience the work environment, and, most importantly, provide extra cash. Have you experienced any gender bias on these jobs? Are you more aware of the problems gender bias causes because of prior experiences of your parents or a family member? Do you think the changes in the work environment that have been brought about by legislation and by changing social views affect you?

As young adults and the future workforce, changes in the work environment will help you. The current improvements and acceptance of atypical career choices will aid you in reaching your career goals. Experiences shared by your parents, family, and friends will prepare you and teach you how to handle difficult work situations. Gender bias in the work place is lessening, society is more accepting of atypical career choices, and employers are more aware of proper work behaviors and practice improved work ethics. All these changes will affect you and some already do. For example, in your current job you may have experienced some sexual harassment from your coworkers. Teens are not always considerate of each other and often use each other's mistakes as reasons to mock or ridicule. In the work environment, this becomes harassment, and you are protected from it.

In addition, as society accepts atypical career choices, more and more schools will make training and education in these fields more accessible. Have you noticed changes in course offerings over the years? You probably have, and these changes are just another example of how changes occurring in the work environment affect you and your peers.

Today a well-paid career with future advancement

opportunities is vital for economic independence. Changing gender roles in the workplace will help make these top-paying careers available to you regardless of your gender. And since our culture is changing its view of the work environment, the choices you make for a career will be more readily accepted.

Changing Roles in the Military

Jerry walked into the mess hall and glanced around. He was getting used to the women in his class. It was kind of a nice change from being in an all-male school. His father, on the other hand, was still furious that women were admitted to the school. Jerry remembered his father's words: "Women have no right in a military academy. They aren't strong enough and they're a distraction."

Looking around, Jerry thought, "Nice distraction!"

Jerry remembered a time not that long ago when he had agreed with his father. When he and the other male students thought the women were only at school to find husbands. How arrogant he and the other male students had been then. He remembered how nasty and cruel he was to the first group of women he met. Jerry looked around and thought, "Wow, things have changed—people have changed."

Jerry and his friends knew now that the female students worked just as hard as, if not harder than, the men. He knew that the women were at the school to learn and were as committed to the goals of the academy as the rest of the student body and faculty.

He learned a lot about women and himself during his academy training and was determined to apply what he learned during his tour of service. Jerry knew these females were still going to meet men who didn't approve of women being in the service. He hoped that he would be strong enough to support the women.

Do any of you know someone in the armed forces? Are they male or female? Chances are the majority of the military people you know are men. This is because the armed forces was the last male-dominated discipline to change.

Women are not new to military service, but at one time, when they did serve, they had to disguise themselves as men. In 1782, Deborah Sampson, (1760–1827), a five-foot-nine-inch twenty-two-year-old, became the first American woman to wear a military uniform. Using the name of her brother, who died at age eight, she enlisted in the Continental Army and served with distinction for a year and a half.

Throughout history, women were excluded from direct combat. They served as nurses, held clerical positions, and taught. Women were delegated to support positions. Even during World War II when there was a severe shortage of doctors, the Army refused to commission women physicians. Until finally in 1943 out of desperation, the Army commissioned female doctors. Women's Airforce Service Pilots (WASPs) flew longer hours, had lower accident rates than the male pilots, and died for their country, but they were not allowed to become members of the armed forces. During times of need due to risks of national security, the presence of women in the military increased. But once the emergency was over, women were expected to return to their homes. Their service and participation during the war effort were forgotten.

Military policy toward women was very slow to change. During the Korean War, women were still holding health-related service jobs and made up only 1 percent of the country's military strength. It wasn't until 1967 that Congress finally removed the 2 percent limit on the number of enlisted women and permitted women to achieve the rank of general or admiral. But even with this legislation, the majority of the U.S. military women serving in the Vietnam War were nurses.

When and how did these conditions change? It began during the Nixon administration in the late 1960s and early 1970s. At that time, the government was considering a plan to replace mandatory military service (the draft) with an all-volunteer force. Several task forces examined military issues that were expected to occur if this change was made. Women's roles were debated because of the fear that there would not be enough qualified men who would volunteer to serve. The task force examining the use of women in the military uncovered and criticized poor treatment and job stereotyping. Changes started to occur. In 1972 1 out of every 30 recruits enlisting was female, but by 1976 this had increased to 1 in 13, and in 1977, the year that ended the first phase of converting to an all-volunteer military, there were 110,000 women on active duty.

During this period, Reserve Officer Training Corps (ROTC) college programs, which train students to become military officers, were opened to women. And in 1975, Congress forced military service academies to admit women too.

Women were making progress opening up this male-dominated institution. But it wasn't easy, fair, or fun for these pioneers. What was it like for these women? How did they deal with the situations they encountered? Why did they choose to join the military knowing how the services felt about women?

How Women Are Treated

Gender roles are constructed by our culture and society. Because of this, culture can either exaggerate or minimize the femininity or masculinity of specific roles. The military has its own set of rules, ethics, structure, philosophy, and function. Military forces are male-dominated mini-cultures with strictly defined gender roles, and like society, they are resistant to change.

That was the environment women faced when they joined the military. New recruits, whether in military academies or in military boot camps, were treated with contempt, humiliated, and sexually harassed.

Military officers did not consider women equal to men. The women were thought of as physically weak, lacking in leadership skills, and a liability. Women slowed military readiness because of pregnancy and family responsibilities. It wasn't until 1975 that Congress forced the military to give women the same family benefits as men. Prior to this, a woman could be discharged if she became pregnant.

The first women accepted to West Point (the U.S. Army's training academy) were required to wear skirts during social functions. At the first school dance, the women, all of whom now had short hair, wore their dress uniforms. School administrators found it disturbing that the women appeared so masculine that couples dancing together looked alike. The Marine Corps, in contrast, required women to wear, at a minimum, lipstick and eye shadow. Also, women were required to take classes in makeup, hair care, poise, and etiquette. These requirements are a deliberate policy used by the Marine Corps to clearly distinguish the women from the men.

Another problem faced by women officers was that of same-sex friendships. The military environment labeled women who developed close friendships as lesbians. Some women turned to sports in order to compensate for the restrictions placed on their friendships. Participation in sports allowed women to build trust and loyal relationships among each other within a safe environment.

Military women overcame many obstacles to prove themselves capable. But even though the women demonstrated they were combat ready, the military still barred their participation in combat duties. What changed this situation?

Combat requires the ability to handle and use weapons. Weapons were heavy and required greater upper body strength. Women did not have this type of strength. Technology altered the need for physical strength. Improvements made by technology provided women the capability to participate in combat. But integration into combat units was slow and unpopular with the general public. It was not until the Persian Gulf War that women's combat abilities were made public. The Persian Gulf War created the political pressure leading to the repeal of the 1948 law that prohibits women in combat aircraft. Why the Persian Gulf War and not any other military action?

Because women were so much a part of the military, it was impossible for the military to ignore their presence when sending troops to the Persian Gulf. Operation Desert Storm was the largest U.S. military action since the Vietnam War. It received heavy media coverage, and quite a bit of that coverage focused on the women. During the Persian Gulf war, there were 537,000 U.S. troops deployed, and 33,300 of them were women who were in important combat support positions. The women directed artillery, fired Patriot missiles, performed construction work, flew airplanes, and refueled tanks. Air Force women maintained and armed combat aircraft while under attack.

Desert warfare made it difficult for the military to define where combat zones were located. This made it difficult to determine which jobs were considered combat jobs (and therefore off limits to women) and which were not. Because of the conditions present during the Persian Gulf War, the concept that women in a war could be kept out of danger was no longer valid. The breakdown of the notion that women could be kept out of danger, the media's publicizing the capabilities of the military women, and women's performance in wartime all led to the acceptance of women in combat.

Women and men, working together in this dangerous and hostile environment, formed relationships that exhibited caring and mutual respect. The media referred to the men and women in the armed forces as a single group in many reports and used the term *service personnel* in place of *servicemen*. These changes helped eliminate the ban against women serving as combat pilots and aboard combat ships, and paved the way for increased acceptance of women in the military.

Women in the military have proven themselves capable of performance levels equal to their male peers, in both academics and service. In June 1995, for the first time in 193 years, the valedictorian of West Point's graduating class was a woman. Statistics for 1993 showed that 12 percent of enlisted service personnel and 12 percent of military officers were women. In addition, although the majority of the positions held by women are in health care, administration, and other traditionally female jobs, an increasing number of women are becoming pilots, navigators, mechanics, engineers, technicians, and military police.

Why Women Choose to Join the Military

If you are a teenage girl, would you join the military? If not, why not? A decision that is right for you may not be correct for someone else. Your personal feelings about military service should not influence your peers' decisions, and vice versa.

Some of you may be thinking that you would not like the strictness of the military. You do not want to be told when to get up in the morning and go to bed at night, or what to do during the day. You may not want to have your free time determined for you by someone who is an authority figure. You might feel that by becoming a member of the military you would lose your freedom of choice. So why do women and men join the military? Why do they want to go through all those hard times? What type of person wants to be told how to live their life?

Women choose to join the military for several reasons. First, there are economic reasons. Typically, when the economy is strong, male unemployment is low. Therefore men are less likely to enlist. However, statistics show a strong economy creates a decrease in the number of available jobs open to women. In contrast, because of the limited number of men enlisting, there are more military job opportunities for women.

Another reason is the promise of a successful future career. Military service provides state-of-the-art technical training and educational opportunities that are usually unavailable to civilians (or available only at a high cost). And for some women, military service becomes a way to escape poverty and to see other parts of the country or other parts of the world.

Whatever the reason a woman has for joining the service, she must work especially hard to achieve her goals. Military life isn't easy and isn't for everyone. But opportunities exist, and some of these opportunities are only available if you are a member of the military. For some women, interest in these opportunities outweighs concern about tackling the unique challenges that will face them in the military.

Conclusion: What the Future Holds

Hearing the garage door open, John looked out the kitchen window and thought, "Good. Maggie's home just in time for dinner."

He was glad that his wife wasn't late; the kids were getting hungry and cranky. It had been a long day. But John knew that when his wife got home, her stories about her workday would entertain the children until dinner was on the table. Feeling glad that Maggie enjoyed her work as the staff veterinarian of an animal shelter and that the kids loved to hear about her job, he returned to finishing dinner.

"Hi, hon. Dinner is almost ready. One story and then all of you come in and sit down!" he yelled as Maggie entered. John heard the kids running downstairs and shouting greetings.

John loved the days he spent taking care of the kids. He would prefer to be home with them all the time but he and Maggie needed the second income that he earned. He was grateful that he and Maggie worked for people who were flexible and allowed the two of them to split up the workweek. John loved their flexible work schedules, and as a bonus, he and Maggie didn't pay for child care because one of them was always with the children.

As he put the final touches on dinner, he thought about how lucky they were. He and Maggie loved their career choices and the way they lived.

Finally, Maggie entered the kitchen, and the whole family sat down to eat.

Maggie and John may not represent the majority of society today. Their way of life is the exception, not the rule. They represent a society that accepts and allows men to stay home and care for the children; a society in which employers are sympathetic and flexible; a society that has gender equality.

Although Maggie and John's situation is out of the ordinary, there are families today that practice gender equality in housework and child care. And in the future, more families will not follow stereotypical gender roles. It is inevitable that change will happen and that gender roles will evolve toward equality. But before this can happen, our culture and society must change.

Home life must offer children both protection and challenge, and it must cultivate gender equality for both sexes. Parents must recognize the most subtle influences they have on gender development and be willing to try to overcome their biases.

Teachers, guidance counselors, and administrators must offer fair and equal treatment of male and female students. Coursework and classroom materials must be unbiased, and students should be free to learn any subject they find interesting without being labeled or ridiculed.

The media has to alter how it portrays masculinity and femininity to give a more balanced and accurate view. It also needs to improve the quality and the subject matter it focuses upon.

More and more men are taking advantage of the Family Leave Act. They are scheduling their jobs so they can help with child care and increasing their participation in family work. These situations teach male children about their gender role. The fathers representing this type of role model are already starting the process of change, and when their children are adults, they in turn will provide appropriate, unbiased role models for their children.

Nothing in life remains the same forever. Change is the one constant you can depend on. But most importantly, before change can occur, society must be made aware of the problem. Slowly, but with certainty, that is happening—and because you chose to read this book, you can help the development of gender equality.

Glossary

abolitionists Members of a nineteenth-century movement in the United States that opposed slavery and worked to gain freedom and rights for slaves.

affirmative action A work environment policy that gives preferential treatment to people who were traditionally discriminated against. This treatment is given in areas including hiring, training, and promotion.

atypical Not usual; out of the ordinary.

coeducational Including members of both sexes.

gender role The behavior, actions, and attitudes expected of and associated with a gender.

hormones Substances in our bodies that affect physical and emotional functions.

hunter-gatherer A member of an ancient form of human society who obtained food by hunting animals and gathering wild plants.

lobbyists People who work to influence elected officials to vote a specific way on legislation.

media Means of communication, including television, radio, newspapers, magazines, and advertising.

nuclear family A traditional concept of a family, made up of two parents and their children.

patriarchal Dominated and governed by males.

propaganda Information, both factual and false, that is distributed to promote or strengthen a cause.

sexual harassment A type of discrimination that involves making sexual advances or demanding sexual favors and withholding or terminating employment or advancement unless these demands are met. Sexual harassment is behavior that creates a hostile, intimidating, or offensive environment for the victim.

suffragists People who work to secure suffrage, or voting rights, for a particular group.

Title IX An act of the U.S. Congress that forbids gender discrimination in any educational program or activity.

Where to Go for Help

American Association of University Women
(AAUW)
1111 Sixteenth Street NW
Washington, DC 20036
Phone: (800) 326-AAUW [2289]
Fax: (202) 872-1425
E-mail: info@aauw.org
Web site: http://www.aauw.org

National Organization for Women (NOW)
P.O. Box 96824
Washington, DC 20090-6824
Phone: (202) 331-0066
Fax: (202) 785-8576
Web site: http://www.now.org

Web Sites

American Men's Studies Association
http://members.aol.com/amsapage

Diversity in Business
http://www.cob.ohio-state.edu/~diversity

Expect the Best from a Girl
http://www.academic.org

Gender Equity in Education
http://www.crpc.rice.edu/CRPC/GT/mborrow/Ge
nderEquity/gendsite.html

The Men's Center
http://www.themenscenter.com

Ms. Foundation
http://www.ms.foundation.org

National Coalition of Free Men
http://www.ncfm.org

National Organization for Men Against Sexism
http://www.nomas.org

National Sons Day
http://pages.prodigy.com/Sons_Day/Welcome.htm

Stereotyping
http://www.ai.mit.edu/people/ellens/Gender/pap/
node6.htm/ #SECTION00310000000000000000

Watch Your Language!
http://www.cs.rice.edu/dcamp/talks/watch-
language.html

For Further Reading

American Association of University Women
 Staff. *Girls in the Middle: Working to
 Succeed in School.* Washington, DC:
 American Association of University
 Women, 1996.

Anker, R. *Gender & Jobs: Sex Segregation of
 Occupations in the World.* Washington, DC:
 International Labour Office, 1998.

Archer, Jules. *Breaking Barriers.* New York:
 Viking, 1991.

Bender, David and Bruno Leone. *Feminism:
 Opposing Viewpoints.* San Diego, CA:
 Greenhaven Press, 1995.

Bender, David and Bruno Leone. *Male/Female
 Roles: Opposing Viewpoints.* San Diego, CA:
 Greenhaven Press, 1995.

Bernikow, Louise. *The American Women's
 Almanac.* New York: Berkley Books, 1997.

Coltrane, Scott. *Family Man: Fatherhood, House-work, and Gender Equality.* New York: Oxford University Press, 1996.

Coontz, Stephanie. *The Way We Really Are.* New York: Basic Books, 1997.

Fanning, Patrick, and Matthew McKay, Ph.D. *Being a Man: A Guide to the New Masculinity.* Oakland, CA: New Harbinger Publications, 1992.

Forsyth, Sondra, and the Ms. Foundation Staff. *Girls Seen and Heard: The Ms. Foundation for Women.* New York: The Putnam Publishing Group, 1998.

Greenspan, Karen. *The Timetables of Women's History.* New York: Simon and Schuster, 1994.

Guernsey, Joann Bren. *Voices of Feminism.* Minneapolis, MN: Lerner Publications Co., 1996.

——*The Gender Gap in Schools.* Springfield, NJ: Enslow Publishers, 1996.

Hite, Shere. *The Hite Report on the Family.* New York: Grove Press, 1994.

Lorber, Judith. *Paradoxes of Gender.* New Haven: Yale University Press, 1994.

Maggio, Rosalie. *The Bias-Free Word Finder: A Dictionary of Nondiscriminatory Language.*

Boston: Beacon Press, 1992.

Mills, Kay. *From Pocahontas to Power Suits.* New York: Plume/Penguin Books, 1995.

Neft, Naomi, and Levine, Ann D. *Where Women Stand.* New York: Random House, 1997.

Nichols, Nancy A., ed. *Reach for the Top: Women & the Changing Facts of Work Life.* Boston: Harvard Business School Press, 1994.

Orenstein , Peggy. *School Girls.* New York: Anchor Books, 1994.

Pipher, Mary, Ph.D. *Reviving Ophelia.* New York: Ballantine Books, 1994.

Pollack, William, Ph.D. *Real Boys: Rescuing Our Sons from the Myths of Boyhood.* New York: Random House, 1998.

Salisbury, Jane, and Sheila Riddell, eds. *Gender Policy and Educational Change.* New York: Routledge, 1999.

Shandler, Sara, ed. *Ophelia Speaks: Adolescent Girls Write About Their Search for Self.* New York: HarperPerennial, 1999.

Shaw, Victoria. *Coping with Sexual Harassment and Gender Bias.* New York: Rosen Publishing Group, Inc., 1999.

Williams, Christine L. *Still a Man's World: Men*

Who Do Women's Work. Berkeley, CA: University of California Press, 1995.

Pamphlet

American Association of University Women.*10 Tips to Build Gender-Fair Schools.* Available from the American Association of University Women, (800) 326-AAUW [326-2289].

Index